DADDY SATURDAY

DADDY SATURDAY

HOW TO BE AN INTENTIONAL DAD TO RAISE GOOD KIDS WHO BECOME GREAT ADULTS

JUSTIN BATT

LIONCREST
PUBLISHING

DADDY SATURDAY

How to Be an Intentional Dad to Raise
Good Kids Who Become Great Adults

ISBN   978-1-5445-0297-7 *Hardcover*

       978-1-5445-0298-4 *Paperback*

       978-1-5445-0296-0 *Ebook*

This book is dedicated first and foremost to God for allowing me to identify the calling he's put me on this earth for and the ability to humbly serve other men on this journey.

To my wife Heather, I'm incredibly grateful that I get to be your husband. While I know I can be "extra" at times (ok...all the time) the person you are makes me a better man and I couldn't imagine doing life with anyone else. Thank you for being an incredible entrepreneur and affording me the opportunity to spend Saturdays with our four children. Daddy Saturday wouldn't be a reality today if it weren't for your commitment to our family and your trust in me. I love you!

To Hayden Olivia Batt, Blane Coleman Batt, Mason Hayes Batt, and Easton Crewe Batt: There are not enough words in the entire English language to describe how much I love you. You are all my heroes! Every day I wake up amazed that I get to be your father. God has a special plan for each of your lives and you will be world changers in the generation that you are alive. I'm honored to steward you along the journey by serving as your guide. I know I tell you this all the time, but I'm proud of you and I love you more than you could ever ask or imagine.

Finally, to my father Dave Batt for setting such an incredible example of what a committed father looks like. I wouldn't be the man I am today without you. To my father-in-law, Scot Reed, for allowing me to marry your daughter and for serving as an additional example of a committed father for me to follow. And to all of the many people, family members, mentors, friends, pastors, coaches, teachers, too many to acknowledge in this book who have poured into my life and helped mold me into the person I am today. Don't for one second ever take for granted the impact you can have on the world around you. Each of you have impacted me in a significant way, and I will take your investment in me and use it to change the future of fatherhood. Thank you.

CONTENTS

FOREWORD

Every generation produces leaders who emerge from the status quo and set a fresh standard for others to consider. That's exactly what Justin Batt is doing in his quest to make "Daddy Saturday" a special day for fathers and their kids.

Justin experienced success in corporate America, but it came with a cost. Not only did his travel cut into the time he could devote to being a great dad, but his wife and the mother of his four children started a business that required her to work on Saturdays. The obvious became a reality. Being supportive of his wife and a committed father to his growing brood, every Saturday Justin would provide the support, nurture, and all-around care for his children.

Justin went all-out in his Daddy Saturday role, and from

his experiences he has catalogued fifty-two ways to encourage your fathering creativity and provide you with practical—and often exciting—ways to get the max out of your Saturday time with your kids. His book outlines this journey. Justin's ultimate goal is to lead an effort to encourage and challenge all dads to make the most of any time they invest in connecting with their kids.

What if all dads were passionate about their fathering? What kind of precedent would that set for the next generation? I'm not sure, but after reading Justin's book we are going to find out.

On the flip side, we do need to realize that fathering, if it isn't prioritized, can slip into a minor role in a man's life. Unfortunately, many men can go for years without really appreciating that their children are only under their care for a short window of time, and then they blink and it's gone. That's an overstatement, but ask any older father if there are issues he wishes he had discussed, events he missed, or things he should have done differently, and his response will remind you how important being a dad really is.

Men, if we fail to make the most of those day-to-day fathering moments, where strong, affirming connections with our kids are being formed, then we can too easily slip into mediocrity, and that just doesn't cut it in the fathering world. Our children deserve better.

Daddy Saturday is a clarion call for millennial dads to step it up—and they must.

If you were gifted with a "good" dad growing up, that's a huge benefit and you can learn from the positive things you saw in him (although none of our fathers were perfect). However, if your dad was absent or distant or harsh with you, then maybe you're longing to fill the void in your heart by being intentional and engaged with your children. Well, guess what? You're on the path to becoming an overcomer father, which will distinguish your legacy and life as a dad. And there's more.

Research clearly supports the notion that children with healthy, involved fathers have higher measures of self-confidence, are less susceptible to peer pressure, and are less likely to drop out of school, engage in risky behaviors, and the list goes on and on. All to say, your kids won't be perfect, but you can give them a foundation that's rich in character and strength—and numerous related positive qualities that are so needed in today's youth.

So, here's the challenge Justin's book brings to you: Pick a few ideas from this book that appeal to you and that are achievable. Try them. Adapt them to your situation. Make them your own, and start a tradition in your fathering journey to have a few regular, predictable things you are going to do that will make a difference.

There are no guarantees, but I can tell you this after watching thousands of dads over the years: if you make these times of connection with your kids a priority, you will be fulfilling one of your God-given roles and, most importantly, you'll provide a legacy for your children and family that will impact future generations.

KEN CANFIELD PHD.
FOUNDER, THE NATIONAL CENTER FOR FATHERING

A NOTE TO MOTHERS, WIVES, AND DAUGHTERS

Have you ever wanted to help your husband or son be a better father, but didn't know how? My hope is this book will be an answer to your prayers as a man speaking to other men about the topic of fatherhood as opposed to a woman, a therapist, or other professional who's not in the practice of day-to-day fatherhood. As you know, men need directions and you are the most likely source for providing the guidance they need. Most men are not going to naturally seek out a book on parenting and relationships nor are they actively asking the question, "How can I be a better father?" I need you to help get this message in the hands of as many men as possible so we can create the momentum needed to impact our current and future fathers and change the trajectory of the next generation of children.

INTRODUCTION

There are many books on fatherhood and parenting from the perspective of a psychologist or academic but very few from a parent who's actually in the mix, fighting the battle to win as an intentional father. That's the space *Daddy Saturday* occupies. The goal of this book is to expand the growing Daddy Saturday movement and destroy one of the root causes of America's societal ills—the spiritual, emotional, and/or physical absence of so many fathers in the lives of their children.

Daddy Saturday seems like a simple enough concept: intentionally engaging our children and maximizing the time we have with them. But it's a real struggle for most dads. Fathers are not nurturers. We are drivers. We are hunter-gatherers with things to do and places to go. It doesn't come naturally for dads to engage kids in the ways kids typically want to be engaged. *Daddy Saturday* is a global movement intended to serve as a catalyst to encourage, motivate, and inspire fathers to engage their children in an intentional way to raise good kids who become great adults.

Before we get too deep into what Daddy Saturday is all about, I need to address something head-on. This book is written for fathers from my perspective as the biological father of four children. However, when I use the term father I'm speaking to whoever plays that role in a child's life. It could be a biological father, adopted father, single mother, father figure, uncle, grandparent...etc. The point here is that intentionality is universal, and as I speak to fathers in this book, I'm speaking to whoever plays that role in the life of a child.

So, what's Daddy Saturday? I have spent almost every Saturday over the past eleven years with my four children accumulating more than 13,000 hours of time engaging my children in planned and purposeful ways on Saturdays. When I saw how much that engagement benefitted my kids, it just made me want to do it even more and spread the word. The Daddy Saturday platform is bigger than just me. It's bigger than my family. Daddy Saturday is about solving the fatherhood crisis in our country. It's about calling all dads to step up, step out, and create a bold vision for their children and their children's future. Disrupting fatherhood is my calling, my passion, my way for changing the next generation, and I'm asking others to join the movement and do the same thing in your household and community.

Listen, this is not about patting myself on the back and boasting about what a great father I am. I don't wear those T-shirts. I'm just a regular guy from a small town in Ohio who never dreamed of writing a book or speaking from a stage. I'm simply a guy who recognized the calling on my life and its ability to help other dads. You know what I want? I want to own my role as a father and raise incredible kids. I want to take a photo of my boys playing football in the backyard...but I also want to put my phone away and engage with them in the moment as all-time quarterback. This is about me helping make sure my children venture off into the world with everything they need to win in life and to help other fathers do the same. This book and this movement are about holding me accountable and helping other fathers overcome the insecurities, overcome the obstacles, overcome the fears we share when it comes to engaging our kids and providing tangible ways to impact their lives and build our own dad résumé of wins.

You may have heard of this concept where a mom observes and compares herself to other mothers on social media and immediately experiences a sense of emotional shaming. These other mothers have their kids perfectly dressed in matching outfits, holding citrus fruit backwards over their eyes, in a dream-home setting where life seems to be perfect. This is how "mom shame" occurs, but dads just don't act that way. A dad doesn't see other fathers on social media and immediately feel emotionally insecure. In fact, dads experience the complete opposite of shame by getting intensely competitive. When a dad sees another father on social media he will say, "I can do more of that, I can do it better, or I will do it faster!" This is actually a positive trait called "dad envy," and it's something I hope to tap into as we walk on this journey together. As you will see, there's nothing I do that you can't do more, better, or faster as a dad. In fact, nothing makes me happier than to see a father take an idea from the Daddy Saturday movement to the next level and share it through our online community.

Fatherhood is at a sour state. There's never been a time where there's more distractions, more demands on us as fathers, or more fractured relationships with our children. If we don't get a handle on how fathers engage their kids, we're going to continue to see very negative consequences in the lives of our children. It all starts with fathers and we are the tip of the spear. This is why the Daddy Saturday movement is needed now more than ever. This movement is pivoting and disrupting the current state of fatherhood so one day we'll look back and say, "We played a significant role in the lives of our children. We changed their trajectory and helped raise good kids who became great adults who are going to be the next generation of fathers and parents to their children and ultimately change the future of our country."

Spoiler alert: I'm not a perfect dad. I've made plenty of mistakes as a father. There are times I get upset and yell at my kids. I let the stress of my environment come out in the way I deal with my children from time to time. I'm not where I want to be as a dad yet, but I'm fighting daily to get there. What I want you to know is if I can do this, you can too. Join the Daddy Saturday movement and get in this fight with me. Fatherhood is no longer a playground, it's a battleground. We as fathers have to rise up and be willing to fight—fight for our marriage, fight for our role as parents, fight against the demands of society, and fight for the future of our children.

What you'll find in *Daddy Saturday* are approaches to engage your kids in intentional ways, ideas for creating epic moments, a new philosophy of parenting, and ways to join the movement individually and in your community. Throughout the book you will find tangible ideas for engaging your children in meaningful ways. The appendix contains an intro to *The Daddy Saturday Playbook* with fifty-two ways—one for each weekend of the year—for dads to intentionally engage their children and create their own Daddy Saturdays. You can visit the free bonus website listed in the book for the full *The Daddy Saturday Playbook* e-book for download. The bonus site also contains a Fatherhood Quiz where you can find out what kind of dad you are and how to best leverage your specific style. You'll also find ideas, updates, speaking dates, and live events on DaddySaturday.com. Last but not least, stay up to date by interacting with us through social media channels.

Daddy Saturday is a global movement that started in my backyard and is now a growing community of fathers. Through the Daddy Saturday Foundation, we've set a lofty goal of impacting ten million men in the next ten years. I'm looking for other men who will step up as fathers and join the fight for fatherhood and our children's future. We can all do a better job as fathers. My hope is this book and the Daddy Saturday movement will inspire you to shift a paradigm in your life, reframe your role as a father, and crush any obstacle holding you back, step-by-step, choice by choice, Saturday by Saturday. If you take what's right in front of you, your kids and your family, apply these principles, and join this movement, I promise you one day you will look back and have written your own incredible story about raising good kids who grew into great adults.

CHAPTER ONE

THE FATHERLESSNESS EPIDEMIC

"When I started studying the issue and issues related to father-lessness, I realized I had all of them. Fear of intimacy, fear of commitment, poor work ethic, just stuff that you don't have when you don't have a man in your life to look you in the eye and say, 'You're good,' or 'Good job.'"

—DONALD MILLER, AUTHOR, FOUNDER OF STORY BRAND

I was standing in the airport terminal at o'dark thirty preparing to board a flight for my corporate job that required me to travel every other week, and I felt like I was having a heart attack. It was as if an 800-pound gorilla were sitting on my chest. I had this overwhelming sense of being trapped in an imaginary box that I couldn't escape. I remember the gate attendant at the counter calling for people with status and thinking to myself, *Not only am I about to have a mental breakdown, but I have the pleasure of sitting in "peasant class" for the next couple of hours.* The gate attendant had made her way through the first fifteen levels of status—titanium, platinum, gold, silver, bronze, diamond, ruby—and I will never forget the man in a suit who made his way to the front of the line. He looked so proud of his status and wore it like a badge of honor. For a split second, I was incredibly envious of his priority position and his status. As you will learn, I often have paradigm shifts hit me like a tidal wave. This one was a tsunami of emotions and crushed me in an enormous way. The voice in my head questioned, *When you look back on your life, do you really want to have the attainment of one or two million airline miles and hotel points on your wall of achievements, and at what cost?* No amount of success can compensate for failure in the home, and I felt like I was a failure. It was at that moment I made the conscious choice to break the chains of tension between work and home that had brought me to the point of anxiety in which I now found myself. I said to myself, *I'm trading my airline miles and hotel points for bedtime stories and baseball games, and I'm not looking back.*

That epiphany was one of many that have occurred over the past ten-plus years, and all of them have led me to become the engaged and intentional father I am today. I still travel for business today and I'm not condemning the lifestyle, however I have a new perspective about the balance between work and home and am far better at managing the tension. I've learned that tension isn't something you will ever eliminate from your life, rather it's something you learn to manage. It's a fight I still work on daily. In fact, less than a year ago, I remember sitting at our twelve-foot-long dining-room table with a pink chandelier overhead inside our 1950s ranch home outside of Charleston, South Carolina. On one side is a long bench where three of our children sit, usually way too close to each other and getting into each other's personal space as we eat. I'm at the head of the table, and Heather and our youngest child are on the other side. I had just returned from a business trip, drove in on two wheels to make it on time for dinner, and my mind was racing with thoughts of the big deal I was working on. I had engaged with my family and the normal flow of the dinnertime routine when I felt that familiar pressure sitting on my chest. As I sat there listening to my kids banter back and forth about school and what Heather had cooked for dinner, I felt the burden again of balancing work and home, wanting to juggle both effectively. When I should have been fully present with my family, I had my phone out on the table—something I never do—and had inadvertently been scanning through a couple of work-related emails and text messages. I was engaged with my phone and not with my family.

It was another paradigm-shifting moment for me. I routinely have my cell phone put away and am engaged and present in the dinnertime conversation. How had I let my guard down and allowed myself to backslide? In the moment I came to a definitive conclusion. I've got such a limited time with my family and my kids, I have the opportunity to decide each and every time I interact with them and set a positive example. Am I going to be engaged and am I going to be intentional, or am I going to let the world and my career and the outside influence distract me from my ultimate mission, which is raising good kids who become great adults?

Looking back on that moment, I realize it was one of those moments many fathers experience: we're with our family but we're not *with* our family. It's like an out-of-body experience where you are there physically but not in spirit. One commonality we all have as fathers is the fact that a long day is a long day regardless of the line of work you are in. After a long day, dinnertime can be one of the situations where tension often occurs, and I recognized in the moment that even though I've been blessed with a great sense of self-awareness, I wasn't really there. After having a mental wrestling match with myself, I zoomed back into the moment, apologized, and put my phone away and engaged my family. As fathers we are all armed with a choice to either own the moment or let it slip away. I won this particular moment, and it served as a building block for future tension battles. The next time you are faced with the tension, recognize it, manage it, and win the moment.

MASCULINITY ERASED

It's a common theme in our home and one of my favorite mental pictures. My boys are running around the house in their underwear with capes flowing from their backs and superhero paraphernalia from head to toe. As they make a lap around the kitchen island I give them all high fives and say, "Hey wildman!" to each one. Where does the phrase "wildman" come from? Deep down in our hearts all men are born to be a wildman and it's what feeds our soul.

Before we dive too deep into the concept of what fatherhood is all about, we must first define what manhood is and should be. Most men don't have a clear sense of what it means to be a man today. Men have lost the appetite for being what they were meant to be: hunter/gatherers, leaders, and heads of their households. So what is manhood? It can be defined as the passage from childhood into adulthood and the demonstration of attributes like courage and strength. In his book *Wild at Heart,* author John Eldridge states, "Deep in his heart, every man longs for a battle to fight, an adventure to live, and a beauty to rescue." We live in such wishy-washy times. All we as men have to do is look around and there are multiple battles to fight at any time. We must fight for our marriages, our role as men and fathers, our faith, our country, and our freedom! Masculinity is under a full frontal assault by the feminist/progressive/intersectional notion that men, manhood, and masculinity are somehow deviant or subject to the withering feminist critique. Men are being emasculated in our culture and in order to set the stage for fatherhood, we as men must realize we don't need to buy into this frail version of manhood. What happens in our society today when young people who got ribbons for participating now have to figure out fatherhood? Being a man and demonstrating the positive characteristics of manhood are not toxic as some might lead you to believe. Rather, embracing the call of the wild and being a man of courage and strength is what society and our children need most.

THE ABSENT FATHER

The absence of strong men in our society is an underlying issue, but it pales in comparison to an epidemic that is the root cause America's societal ills that's called father-lessness. Fatherlessness takes on two different forms: absenteeism and presenteeism. According to the United States Census Bureau, 19.7 million children, more than one in four, live without a father in the home.[1] Those who live without a father in the home have a four-times

---

1   National Fatherhood Initiative, "Fatherhood Absence + Involvement Statistics," From 2017 US Census Bureau, https://www.fatherhood.org/fatherhood-data-statistics

greater risk of poverty. They're seven times more likely to become pregnant as a teenager. They're more likely to have behavioral problems. They're more likely to abuse substances like drugs and alcohol. They're more likely to go to prison. They're two times more likely to suffer from obesity, commit crime, and drop out of high school. This is not to disparage single moms, who go far above and beyond the call of duty to raise children, the vast majority of whom are great contributors to society. But the absence of a father breaks the family dynamic. The importance factors of fathers are proven.

But the purpose of this book is not to impact the lack of a father in a home, which requires a societal shift and cultural challenge that is beyond our scope here. This book is directed at fathers who are physically present but emotionally absent. And while we don't have a lot of statistics to show the number of unengaged fathers in a home and the impact it brings, what we can show is the amount of time fathers are spending with their children in engaged, intentional situations are declining day over day, year over year, because of all the demands and pressures in society today. Intentionality in parenting can simply be defined as being deliberate with the time you have with your children.

Time is the greatest gift you can give your children, but the average father spends less than two hours a day with their children, according to the National Bureau of Labor Statistics, so the importance of being intentional during that short period of time, every single day, is paramount.[2] Paradoxically, the time decreases on the weekend when we'd expect to see that time go up. There are so many demands on fathers during the week that the bandwidth, the energy, the mindfulness, and the will power is gone by the time they get to the weekend. There's no gas left in the tank and it's very difficult to be engaged with your kids at that point.

I know at the end of a week—at the end of a day—my willpower is spent. I've made so many decisions, for myself and for others, that I've got very little left, and it's very easy at that point to give in to what feels good, which may not be what matters most, and there's a big difference between what feels good and what matters most. What feels good may be sitting down to watch the football game. It may be going to play golf and having a few beers with the boys. That certainly feels good at the time, and it's great for fathers to go refresh themselves in those ways. There's nothing wrong with taking time for yourself and recharging your batteries as long as it's truly going to re-energize you. However, it's also equally as important to have the mindfulness to say, "Is that the highest and best use of my time?" When I look at the scale

2   National Bureau of Labor Statistics, "American Time Use Survey Summary," US Department of Labor, June 28, 2018, https://www.bls.gov/news.release/atus.nro.htm

of the time that I have with my kids, is there a way that I can balance that out a little bit and make the hard decision to be intentionally engaged by planning something meaningful with my children?

One of the reasons fathers struggle with proactively engaging their children is because behaviors don't follow feelings, feelings follow behaviors. Let's just be honest for a minute. There are times I don't feel like making the investment to plan something that fully engages my children. There are times where I feel like just showing up and figuring it out on the fly or checking out and letting them occupy themselves with technology. It's the same thing when you look at exercising or working out. I try to work out early in the morning, but there are many times that I don't feel like it. In fact, I rarely feel like getting out of bed early and going for a run, but I find that once I get into it and engage in the behavior, the endorphins start to kick in, I'm in the moment, and then the feelings of positivity start to follow. It's the same principle when it comes to engaging your kids—the feelings will follow the behaviors, and in the words of Nike, "Just do it!"

Here's the payoff for being present both physically and mentally that stands in stark contrast to the earlier story: On a recent weekday evening I was sitting at the head of our dining-room table fully engaged, playing a game of TableTopics with Heather and our four children. Table-

Topics is a game comprised of a box containing a bunch of cards that have a question on one side. In our family, I always read the question and each person takes a turn answering the question from their point of view. There are no right or wrong answers, and it's an incredible way to learn your children's perspective on many topics. This has been a game changer for our family during dinnertime to create intentional conversation. One particular evening, when asked to name the best thing about each family member, my four-year-old, Easton, finally answered with something other than a bodily function.

"The best thing about Mommy is her booty," he said, as everyone howled.

"Hey, that's my line!" I responded with mock anger (we know who he learned that from!).

At one point, I zoomed out for a minute like an objective bystander and saw myself sitting there with this incredible family that I've been blessed with, fully engaged, fully present, creating a memory that we will have for a long time. The smiles and amount of laughter around our table in that moment will stick in my mind forever, and I realized I had begun to achieve the level of status I was searching for. My kids' answers are often so funny that two of them are spitting milk out of their nose and falling off the table because we're all laughing so hard.

It's probably an unreasonable expectation to say every dinner is going to be like so entertaining, but what I can tell you is because I was engaged, because we had a plan (TableTopics), we've created many memorable experiences around our dinner table. The key was being intentional and having something to help stimulate the conversation. We weren't just going through the routine of eating dinner. We were creating an experience and an environment we could all be engaged in intentionally.

DADDYING BY DEFAULT

When I speak about my purpose to make dads more intentional and raise good kids who become great adults, a lot of people often expect to hear some story about how I didn't have a father in the home, or my dad wasn't engaged, or he was one of those traveling salesmen who left on Monday, came back on Friday, and golfed with his buddies on Saturday. And that just wasn't the case. I had a very engaged father. That doesn't mean he was perfect, because there were certain things that were important to him, like maintaining the car, the yard, or the home that would take up his time, so sometimes we would come second, but there was always time for us. If I ever asked my dad for anything, he was there and committed to it. I want to thank him for setting an example and giving me a strong platform to jump off of. Maybe you are like me and you had an engaged father and your goal is to take the example he set and take it to the next level with your kids. If this describes you, then the information in this book will be a catalyst to get you there. On the other end of the spectrum, maybe your dad wasn't there for you or maybe you didn't even have a dad growing up. I know a guy whose father was a pimp and had twenty-three kids. He was raised on welfare by his mother and his father wasn't involved in his life. As a father of four beautiful children of his own, he wants to give them everything he never had. If you identify with the story above and your father was absent, the information, encouragement, and application you find in this book and the Daddy Saturday movement will allow you to create a new branch of your family tree.

My wife Heather is in the bridal industry, and I continuously hear stories about how brides have dreamed about what their wedding day would be like since they were a young girl. When I say what their wedding day will "be like," I don't mean general details of the day—these girls have thought about the exact details like the color of the flowers, to the type of dress, what's on the menu, and who they are going to marry! Let's face it, most men don't dream about what their wedding day will be like when they're younger like women do, down to the little details. Many men also approach fatherhood the same way and don't think about exactly what the experience of being a father is going to be like. We typically just react to the situation and go with the male instinct ingrained within us. Shoot from the hip, as I like to say. We as men could learn a little bit from these brides and begin thinking about the specific details of our role as fathers. While it would certainly help to begin this process before you become a father, you may be like me and be in the middle of fatherhood. I was certainly shooting from the hip for a period of my fatherhood journey, and it wasn't until I took an inventory of my approach to fatherhood and thought, *What do I know about being a father? What do I know about what great fathers are like? What do I know about what bad fathers are like? What do I have in my personal memory bank from either my own experiences or other fathers I know? Where are the knowledge gaps?* At this point I've spent countless hours assessing the details of my fatherhood journey, read many books on the topic, and interviewed experts in the field of fatherhood. Due to the fact you are reading this book, you are already taking a huge step toward focusing on your fatherhood journey. Take some time to make your own assessment of where you are as a father and where you want to be in the future. Through the course of this book we will continue to walk together along the path of fatherhood, and while our situations may look different, our destinations are all the same.

DAD ON SATURDAY

My journey to be an intentional dad really didn't start until we had our first daughter, Hayden Olivia, on November 21, 2007. I recognized that, like most young parents, I had this beautiful new baby in front of me, and I knew nothing about how to be a parent outside of what I had been exposed to from my parents. We received more training when we picked up our Bernedoodle puppy "Weekend" from the breeder than we did any of our children. Unlike a new gadget, she didn't come with a handbook! (I tend not to read directions anyway!) So, I drew on my faith, on wisdom from the Bible, read books and listened to podcasts from digital mentors who are fathers, and I looked at examples from my own life of great fathers. I decided to do some R&D, which stands for rip-off and deploy, to see what I could take from them and then implement in my own life as a father.

Like many parents, I didn't have much of a chance to warm up to the practice of fatherhood. Heather was a teacher, and even though she has an incredible heart for children, she felt the calling to move on from teaching. I left for a business trip and suggested she develop a business plan for what she wanted to do, and I would support her. After doing some research, she decided it was going to be babies or brides. I liked the idea as you have birth, death, and marriage in between, so bridal is a little bit of a recession-proof industry. Looking into it a little more, we also felt that there was too much noise in the baby realm, and it was a tough market to penetrate. Not long after the birth of Hayden Olivia, she launched her bridal business, naming it in her honor, Hayden Olivia Bridal. Being an entrepreneur in the retail industry, Saturdays are always the busiest, which left me alone with Hayden Olivia from the time she was only two weeks old.

At first, I would just stare at my beautiful baby girl and wonder what we were going to do for the next eight to ten hours together. Eventually, Hayden Olivia just blended into whatever I had going on for the day, even Clemson football tailgate parties. I can remember doing things around the house, and as she got older she would follow me around in one of those little walkers. I would put silly hats on her and dress her in funny outfits to take photos that I would send to Heather just to let her know that we were having fun. One of our favorite activities was to put on music and dance. I wouldn't say it was easy, but one or two naps a day certainly allowed for me to have a bit of my own time during our days together. It wasn't a "Daddy Saturday" at that point, but a Saturday with Dad.

AND THEN THERE WERE FOUR

The game changer occurred when Blane came along on November 19, 2009. That's when it got a little more challenging and the perspective of fatherhood really shifted for me. Two children required a lot more intentionality. Before, Hayden Olivia would just fit into my plans. Now, I had to figure out how I was going to handle both of them and take things to the next level. At first, it was just taking care of their basic needs—and infant children have basic needs ALL the time. But it quickly became apparent to me that I couldn't hang out at the house all day, especially after Mason came along two years later. Sure I wanted it to be a fun day for my kids, but I also wanted it to be a pleasurable experience for myself, and frankly those were some of the most stressful and uncomfortable times as a dad. I am a Type A personality. I'm very disciplined and routine-oriented, because that's how my brain works. I'm intentional with my life and plan things out in advance. But, man, when you have kids, throw that all out the window, especially when you have multiple kids and some are infants. I can remember just the sheer amount of effort to get out the door to go somewhere. That's probably why most dads don't do it. Just to go to the grocery store was a major production—the feeding, the dressing, the packing. We had to have diapers and a diaper bag and a spare bottle or two, as well as wipes and toys. There's getting everybody in the car and the buckling into the car seats. It's a monumental effort just to go do something routine like going to the grocery store.

You also just have to plan for the unplanned when you're in those moments. Mike Tyson once said, "We all have a plan until you get punched in the face." I think that's how it is with kids and being a father. You can have the best-laid plans, but eventually, you're going to get punched in the face by the circumstances of having children, like a temper tantrum in the middle of the store. There are plenty of times where I let those situations get the best of me and let it dictate the rest of our day. I learned the lesson of pivoting by not allowing the stressful parenting circumstances to dictate my contentment with our time together on Saturdays. As a parent, you just have to let stuff go and pivot, and sometimes those pivots turn out to be the best moments.

I can remember more than once asking before we left the house, "Did everybody go to the bathroom?" And then we're in the middle of Lowe's and one of the kids says, "Daddy, I gotta go to the bathroom, and I gotta go now!" Now you've got to take three or four kids into the men's bathroom, which typically is not the cleanest at a home improvement store. "Don't touch anything! Keep your hands off the toilet lid! Just stand there!" You've got a baby on your chest, then one kid washes their hands and now they all want to wash their hands. It's fun to play in the water, put soap on your hands, and stick your head under the hand dryer!

I can remember more than one "blowout diaper" and having to leave a cart in the middle of the grocery store, walk out to the car, and change the diaper. The other kids are all there climbing all over the car while I'm changing a child on the back of the tailgate. It's a thirty-minute process just to make it all work. I can see why dads don't do it. It's difficult. I just had to find humor in the situation and realize it's just part of life as a parent. Looking back, I wouldn't trade those moments and hilarious memories and the growth I had as a parent. My kids remember those early days and our time together. They don't always remember exactly what they did, but I have the pictures and the scars to prove it! The takeaway is even though your kids are young, there is a strong developmental factor in the fact they knew that Dad was physically there.

One thing I remember the most from those early days are the reactions of others, women mostly, to seeing a dad with three or eventually four kids—the youngest, Easton, came along in 2014—when I'd be out running errands, and the looks and responses of people reacting to a dad by himself with all of his kids. I'd be pushing a shopping cart with Easton in a Baby Bjorn carrier on my chest, one or two in the cart with all the groceries, another hanging off the cart. It was a sight to see. People loved to engage me and ask, "How many kids do you have? Well, you know how that happens, right?" And we'd all get a good chuckle. It happened so often that eventually I made up a new answer: "Yes, my wife can't keep her hands off of me," which created an even better response. To this day, I still love to say that, especially in front of Heather and watch her face turn red, which it does every time I say it, even though she knows it's coming.

DADDY SATURDAY GENESIS

Why is it not the norm to see a father on a Saturday by himself with his kids, even doing something as routine as going to the grocery store? Early on, Dad on Saturday was simply me spending Saturday with my children and engaging in what most would call routine activities. Over time, we decided to take things to a whole new level, which is how the term "Daddy Saturday" came about. The genesis has two major components.

The first was when Hayden Olivia was just about four years old. Heather and I have made it a priority to have a date night sans kids at least once per month. This practice has been such an important pillar in our marriage and has helped enhance our communication and connectedness. I had been thinking about how I could do something special with Hayden Olivia to engage her one-on-one just like I do with Heather, so I decided to do a daddy-daughter date night. This was my way of not only spending time with her, but also teaching her how a great guy should act. You know, the things of days past like manners and respect. The first daddy-daughter date night was a quick trip to a restaurant called Toast in downtown Charleston where I knew they had good buttered noodles, which was her favorite dish, along with a Shirley Temple. It was a fun, quick experience that I felt was the start of something special. I wanted it to be more, so for the second daddy-daughter date night a month later, we got dressed up in our Sunday best. She was in a beautiful dress, red and blue with white polka dots. I wore a jacket and tie. I didn't really have a formal plan but figured there were so many good restaurants in Charleston, we'd find something that would work for our evening together. We had just gotten downtown and started walking when the sky literally opened up, and it started pouring buckets as soon as we walked out into the street. I'd forgotten to bring an umbrella, so I proceeded to do what any gentleman would do: I took off my jacket and I held it above her head until we could seek refuge and ducked under some awnings. We had skipped about two awnings down until we came across an Italian restaurant. "Italian...perfect," I muttered to myself, because I knew they'd have noodles. We walked in and were delightfully surprised at the sound of a live five-piece jazz band playing in the lobby. There was really no one in the place because it was early for dinner. I asked for the best table in the house. We did a quick dance on the way up the stairs to our table. She seated us right at the window looking down over the Charleston Market.

I was quite nervous about the date in the first place, because what do you talk about with a three-year-old?

Is she going to like it? Is she going to remember this? Is she going to enjoy the conversation? But it turned out great. I'll never forget my daughter ordering plain noodles with a hint of butter and a Shirley Temple. I ordered a fabulous meal. I watched her slurp noodles one at a time and chuckled to myself as I thought, *Oh, sweetheart, please do that on your first date.* I taught her the important stuff, like how to put the napkin on her lap, drink with her pinky out, and eat the cherry in her drink without using her hands. The dinner conversation seemed to flow easily, and I remember thinking it wasn't nearly as difficult as I thought it was going to be.

We finished dinner, walked downstairs, and headed next door to Ben & Jerry's for dessert. It had stopped raining. People started to come back out around the marketplace. We were sitting on a bench, enjoying our ice cream with Hayden Olivia swinging her feet back and forth when I felt the crinkle of the receipts in my pocket. I pulled them out and said, "Oh, my goodness. I spent $70 on dinner with my daughter." Then it hit me like a shockwave and my perspective changed completely. *You didn't just SPEND $70 on dinner with your daughter. You just INVESTED $70 in the life of your daughter.* And what a great investment it was. It was one of those moments that just really shook me as a father, because I was intentional. I didn't have an exact plan, but I took the time to do a date night with my three-year-old daughter. We had an incredible experience, a memory burn that I will remember forever and that she still talks about to this day. We created a legacy from one experience.

The emotions I felt from that first date night with Hayden Olivia started to grow inside, and I wanted more experiences like that with my children. Recognizing if I wanted to create more experiences like date night, then I had to have a game plan and be intentional in my approach to the time with my children. Now, fast forward to having four children and realizing on those Saturdays, alone by myself, I could put together a game plan each Saturday and make the day a special one for me and my kids. It was very important I didn't loaf my way into a Saturday. As I began to engage my kids on those Saturdays, I didn't realize it at the time, but I was creating a set of standards or a baseline for what they expected from me. I knew we were onto something when about the middle of the week my kids would ask me, "Hey dad, what are we doing on Saturday?" There was a sense of anticipation and excitement for our day together. Then one morning at breakfast, one of the kids, I believe it was Mason, mashed it all up and said, "Dad, what are we doing for *Daddy Saturday?*" I almost cried when he said it, and I knew this was the theme for our day together. We've been calling them Daddy Saturdays ever since.

CHAPTER TWO

BLESSING OR BURDEN MINDSET

"I prayed for this child, and the Lord has granted me what I have asked of him."

1 SAMUEL 1:27

"Having a two year old is like having a blender, you just don't have a top for it."

—JERRY SEINFELD, COMEDIAN

I had just completed a long Daddy Saturday with the kids. It was late in the day and we had been going at it since early in the morning. The kids were back inside resting and we were all pretty tired from our escapades that day. I was the last man standing and as I walked around the house, I saw toys strewn from one end to the next. I started picking them up, and by the tenth toy, I started to think to myself, *Why am I out here doing this? Where are my kids? They should be out here helping me. Isn't that why I had four kids in the first place, so that I didn't have to do all this by myself?*

I was viewing each of those toys as a burden and feeling the pain in my back as I bent down to pick up each one and looking at all the others I still had to put away. And then I had one of those lightning-bolt moments where I had yet another perspective shift. As a man of faith, I believe that God put this thought in my head. *Justin, you've got a choice: you can look at situations in life like they're a blessing or a burden and you can view your children the same way.* My perspective immediately shifted, and each one of those toys then became a blessing as they were visual reminders of the epic day I just finished with my kids. It wasn't about the mess of toys in the yard. It was about recognizing in every moment we always have a conscious decision to make in our minds about our children and how we're going to view them. Are we going to be grateful for our children and realize how lucky we are or are we going to be ungrateful and view them as a problem? Possessing a blessing verses a burden mindset is critical because every time we have an interaction with our kids, if we're mindful, we can move the relationship forward and respond in a loving way.

We just put a pool in our backyard, and there's a large area of new sod between our home and the pool. When the sod was first laid, the grass was green and thick. However, over a period of about two weeks, I began to notice a path in the sod. The area where the kids ran from the house to the pool had become trampled down and began turning brown. At that point I had two options: either redirect their path to a new area and allow the sod to recover or put in hardscape and not worry about maintaining the sod. The process in our brains as it relates to the neural pathways that form in our thinking is exactly the same as the sod in my backyard. Over time, each decision we make adds up to form neural pathways that determine how we respond or react to certain situations, like disciplining our children. If we choose to respond with a blessing mindset over and over, we can actually form a highway of positive thinking in our minds through the development of neural pathways. We can also go the other direction and form a highway of negative thinking by reacting with a burden mindset.

Like most dads after a long day at work, I can be a little revved up when I walk in the house, which is usually full of kids running around after being sedentary in school all day. I'm extremely extroverted, and I'm speaking to people and surrounded by people all day. When I get home, part of how I like to recharge is by spending time with Heather and my kids one-on-one. However, this rarely happens as I get attacked the moment I walk in the door and it's "Dad, can you come play football?"

"Dad, come jump on the trampoline!" "Dad, help me with my homework!" It's in that moment I have a decision to make: am I going to treat their request as a blessing or a burden? One thing that's helped me immensely is letting go of my expectations for what I want to happen the moment I walk in the door. Although it seems trivial, by letting go of my expectations I now have the freedom to respond to whatever the dynamic is when I walk in the door rather than react to what I thought it should be. If I may also offer advice to the married men reading this: If you want to dramatically improve your marriage, not only do you need to let go of your expectations, but you also need to completely rid yourself of all criticism. When we were first married our home had carpet just off the main living area. When I came in the front door I could visibly see if there were carpet lines in the floor from Heather vacuuming. If I failed to point out the carpet lines on my own she would say, "Notice anything?" Fast forward years later, if I say anything critical toward Heather, she will often respond, "Carpet lines!" I've learned no one has ever changed based on criticism they received so I've made the decision to eliminate criticism from my marriage and role as a father. Not easy, but necessary. It's through conscious decisions like turning criticism into affirmation or changing your thought process from burden to blessing that we are able to create the positive neural pathways in our brains allowing us to naturally respond in the moment.

Being a father who wins is 80 percent mindset and 20 percent action. To be a successful father, I found I have to create those positive pathways, so that over time I can respond and react to my children in the appropriate way. As I've pointed out in Chapter One, feelings follow behavior, and that's really critical to understand because oftentimes I may not feel like engaging with my children, but once I begin doing it, the feelings of wanting to engage my children will tend to follow. You can't wait on the feeling or you'll be waiting a long time. It starts with the right mindset and ends with taking action.

Mel Robbins wrote a book called *The Five Second Rule* in which she says the way the human brain is wired, when you have a thought you literally have five seconds to act on a decision; otherwise, it becomes just a fleeting thought. If you wake up in the morning and think, *I need to get out of bed and work out*, you only have those five seconds to act on that thought and get out of bed. If you don't, chances are you'll hit the snooze button and won't do it.

It's the same thing with parenting—you've got to act on an impulse to engage your kids right away or you'll hit the parenting snooze button and say to yourself, *I'll do it later*. You might have the best of intentions, but it's not likely to happen. The more you act on the impulse, the easier it will get, too, because you're reprogramming and training your brain to react in a positive way.

It's human nature to react rather than respond, so it's also critical to understand your personality style and how you react. From my experience there are two personality types, exploders and imploders. I tend to be an exploder. I have a really high intensity, high personal velocity. People with this personality style tend to have triggers that set them off and cause them to react. I've found an exploder can benefit from a form of recognition when they get triggered, so I wear two orange motivational rubber bracelets on my right wrist. One is by a brand called Active Faith and the other is from a group called Focus 3, and it states $E + R = O$, which means we can't control the events that happen in our lives, but we can control our response, and that determines the outcome. A lot of times I'll either look at my wrist and stop or I'll pull the bands and snap them against my wrist as my key to be mindful of my reaction. That's the reminder to say, *Calm down, think about this before you engage.* Heather will often remind me if she sees my intensity level escalating and say, "Hey, Justin, snap your wrist." Accountability is great—having someone there who can see it from the outside because it's hard to see it yourself sometimes.

On the flip side of the exploder is the imploder. This type of personality tends to become more introverted, holds their emotions inside when they get mad, and has a more passive-aggressive type of behavior. This personality type requires similar self-awareness, but it tends to be more of a process than an impulse like the exploder. The introvert needs to say, "I'm starting to smolder here. I'm holding this internally. I'm building bitterness and resentment toward my children or toward the situation. I've got to be able to express this in a positive way to get it out because if I hold it in, that's not healthy."

Regardless of your personality type, it goes back creating positive neural pathways. Each and every time you engage in a certain behavior, good or bad, you're literally creating a pathway in your brain that says, "This is how I'm supposed to react." and it becomes more and more ingrained. It becomes easier and easier to react that way because you've trained yourself to do it.

But if you do overact, which we all do from time to time, the biggest thing is to have mindfulness to see your mistake and apologize. "Hey, I overreacted here. That's not the way that Daddy should have responded. I wish I would have responded differently. Can you forgive me?" It's having the awareness to come back and admit your mistake. Showing your deficiency in front of your kids is an incredible gift in and of itself.

DAILY SELF-REFLECTION

There's a great quote from Tony Robbins (no relation to Mel): "You're not going to change until your shoulds become your musts." It's very easy to say, "Well, I *should* not get angry with my kids. I *should* be able to control my temper." I *should*, I *should*, I *should*. It's critical to win each of those moments and it starts with evaluating yourself, whether it's in the morning with all the chaos of getting to school or at night after a hard day at work and say, "Did I respond in the way that was me at my absolute best?" I found myself continuing to fall short in those moments, and it wasn't until I was sick and tired of being sick and tired of my responses that my should became a must and I changed. Self-evaluation and self-coaching are critical skills every father needs in order to win the daily inter-actions with their kids.

Some sort of deep-rooted insecurity as fathers, coupled with the stresses of life and career, might explain why we don't respond correctly. In our home we have the Four Ds of Discipline: Disrespect, Dishonest, Destructiveness, and Disobedience. I can think of a time recently where I came home and wasn't at my best. I was stressed out from my work day, and I walked in the house and I heard my boys going crazy in their bedroom, which they had just destroyed. Instead of just being calm and saying, "Guys you know the Four Ds, this is not what we do. You need to have responsibility for your things, and you're clearly showing me that you don't."

Instead of doing that, I walked in and felt the triggers

of disrespect, destructiveness, and disobedience. In fact, most of the time it's not even what my kids were doing that causes me to get angry. It's their reaction demonstrating a lack of respect or remorse for what they've done that causes me to become angry. I ended up raising my voice, and I even kicked one of the toys into the closet. Not good. I completely lost my temper. It was so ridiculous looking back on it, but I recognized the fact that it had nothing to do with my kids and their toys being scattered everywhere. I overreacted because I was stressed out about work, and yelling and kicking a toy was my way of taking it out on my children because I felt disrespected. Isn't it so much easier to react to our circumstances and take the negative environment we're in and apply it to a person? What a complete moment of failure. I don't want my kids thinking I'm a rage monster, and they clearly don't know or understand the fact that I had a stressful day at work. Instead of making excuses for my bad behavior I decided to take the necessary steps so I wouldn't react this way in the future. As we've discussed, I've learned to release my kids from expectations of how they are going to respond when they are disciplined, and I'm learning to focus on the problem and not the person. It works much better to say, "Boys, the problem is you agreed to have your room cleaned before bed each night and based on what I'm seeing, you're going to be in here for a while." I'm constantly searching for the problem and using it as leverage to respond appropriately.

Why does this matter? It matters because you build your relationship with your kids in small steps. The job of parenting is not done in one big fell swoop; it's made in those incremental moments. You have to look at each one of those situations with the blessing versus the burden perspective. Did you enhance or detract from the relationship? Did you move it forward or backward? Every time you view them as a blessing, you're more likely to respond appropriately and move the relationship forward. If you do this the right way when they're young, it sets the foundation for when they get older, when they're a teenager and something big occurs. All those little moments add up. When you've made all those deposits over the years and set all the right pathways in your mind, it's so much easier to then respond the appropriate way when it really, really matters. I'm learning to take every opportunity and small opening my kids give me to engage them in conversation. This most often comes in the form of "Dad, can you help me with something?" When I hear those words, I jump at the chance to engage because I know those moments could be fleeting as my kids enter their teenage years and adulthood. I don't ever want to create a situation where my kids think they are bothering me or I'm critical in my response, because the older they get, the higher the stakes of the conversation, and I want to be there as a guide when it matters most.

I heard a story of a father putting an envelope in his

daughter's car that had the insurance information, the registration, and a AAA card, along with a note that read, "If you're reading this, you've likely been pulled over for speeding or you've been in an accident. I just want you to know that the most important thing to me is that you're okay, and I love you. I'm here for you. Call me if you need me." When the girl got into an accident and pulled out the contents of the envelope to give them to the officer, while her dad wasn't there, he had preempted himself to respond appropriately because of the letter, so now when his daughter called, the interaction was completely different than, "I can't believe you got in an accident and wrecked the car!" This father is a genius because he's already said the right thing to his daughter before she even calls. He's told her he loves her, the car isn't as important as she is, and he's there for her. The tone of the call will be completely different than if she's calling wondering how Dad will respond and if he's going to blow his lid. Before any conversation I want my kids to feel in their hearts and minds what the content of the envelope said, I love you, you are more important to me than any material thing and I'm here for you. How you get there is through daily deposits as you respond to your kids in the seemingly mundane situations of everyday life.

As you advance through the stages of parenting you will find that your role evolves over time. When your kids are young you will be in training mode. This is when you are firm with them or even yell at them if appropriate, like when they're about to ride their bike out into the street or touch something that's hot. In that moment it's completely appropriate to yell at them at the top of your lungs because you're saving their life or preventing a serious injury. After the training phase you will move into the teacher phase of parenting. This is where you not only say don't do that, but now you also explain why. An example I often find myself discussing with my kids is it's not that you can't do something as much as should you be doing it? The fact that I have four kids who are split between the training and teaching phases of parenting is one of the biggest challenges I face. It's easier and more convenient to tell my older kids no as a training parent, but that's not the response they need or deserve. The third phase of parenting as I see it is where I one day long to be as a wise old sage. This is the phase of parenting where they come into my office late one night as a teenager or call me from college and say, "Dad, can I talk to you about something?" I dream of these moments as a parent; however, I've come to realize that I will only be allowed to become the wise sage if I handle the training and teaching opportunities well when my kids are young. The more they begin to see me as a provider of wisdom now, the more likely we will continue that relationship into the future.

So how do you practically apply these principles and get yourself in a frame of mind to respond appropriately? One of the ways I've been able to retrain my brain to respond in the right way is by taking a few minutes when I pull in the driveway after work to meditate and prepare myself so that when I walk in, I win in the moment and the situation. I've got to prepare my mind for the situations because if I don't, my lizard brain and those visceral reactions will likely come out.

Visualization is another tool, picturing in your mind what it looks like to walk in the house and engage your wife and kids in an appropriate way after a stressful day. I know it may sound a little silly, but if you visualize it, you've got a much better chance of your vision actually happening. The alternative is jumping out of your car, flying into the house, getting whacked upside the head, and reacting without thinking. Trust me. It works. Athletes and other professionals use visualization all the time to improve their performance. Dads can, too.

Blessing or burden. The choice is up to you. When your kids are young the days might seem so long, but the years are so short. You've probably had people say to you, "Don't blink or you will miss your kids growing up!" It's such a true statement, and it caused me to search for a way to visually have a reminder of my kids' time in the home.

We have four glass jars of pebbles side by side on the fireplace mantle in the house with each pebble representing a week that the kids are in the home until age eighteen. That's 936 pebbles at the start when they're born, and what's shocking is that Hayden Olivia's jar is more than halfway empty. She's halfway out of the house already, and that visual reminder is a huge motivator because it really helps to see how limited your time is with them. There's an also an app from Parent Cue I recommend that also shows the number of days your child has left in the home. The days are so long but the years are so short. The years—and the opportunity to impact your kids and build the foundation and framework for them to be good kids who become great adults—really are so short. Let's make the most of them.

CHAPTER THREE

MARGIN MATTERS

"Margin is the space between our load and our limit."

—RICHARD SWENSON, M.D., AUTHOR AND
CULTURAL MEDICINE RESEARCHER

As a father, there are times when you may feel like you can't catch your breath. There always seems to be more to do than the time to do it. We've all seen the coffee mugs and T-shirts speaking about the need for twenty-five hours in a day. Contrary to what seems to be public opinion, maybe it's not a lack of time, but rather a lack of setting the right priorities. The next phase of being an exceptional father is protecting the margin in your life. The margin I'm speaking of is the kind that can provide an allowance or space for you to be an engaged father to your children. In today's fast-paced society, it's very easy to burn the candle at both ends and get to the point where you're stretched in so many areas, it's difficult to be the best father you can be. We're stretched professionally, financially, physically, mentally, and socially. It's very easy to get to the point where your bandwidth is so strained that you just have very little left when you get home at the end of the day or when you get to the weekend.

Warning: When you read what's next, please don't judge me, or in the words of Jon Acuff, don't compare your beginning to my middle. I'm weird and Heather and kids tell me so all the time. It's who I am and how I'm wired. You don't need to do exactly what I do to create margin in your life, but you can absolutely take the cornerstone principles and apply them to your life in the way that works for you.

It's vital you have awareness of the margin in your life and create an allowance for intentional time with your children. Examine your current schedule and pace and be honest with yourself. Are you creating margin so that when you enter the home at the end of the day or when you get to the weekend, you're not burned out and have nothing left? Even for someone who has a high personal velocity, if your RPM gauge is constantly in red, there's going to be a breakdown. There has to be a conscious effort to plan your ideal week and create periods during the day to create that margin. When I speak, one of the most common questions I'm asked is "what's your morning routine?" I'd like to share how I start my day as a few simple practices have changed my life, and perhaps you can take some of what I do and change your life too. I like to get up early in the morning to do a couple of things that help me create margin in my day. I wake up between 4:30 and 5:00 a.m., make a hot tea and do a devotional, and spend some time in prayer and meditation for about thirty minutes. By 5:30, I'm dressed and out the door for a four-mile run and then come back and work out in the gym in our backyard pool house. By 6:15 or so I'm in the house eating breakfast, getting Heather coffee, waking the kids up, and helping them get ready for school. Mornings used to be such a chaotic and stressful time for our family. It's still chaos, but it's more of a controlled chaos now and my morning routine has changed the game for both me and my family. I've already created margin by frontloading my day, and now I have space to operate in. While there are four lunches and four book bags to pack, homework to sign off on, breakfast to eat, clothes to iron, and hair to style, I have the time to engage my kids and help Heather during an extremely chaotic time in our household. As we are getting ready I often like to ask the kids what their goal is for the day, and then follow-up with them during dinner to see if they accomplished it. Most of the time it's something simple like not talking in class or getting a good grade on a test. By getting up early and running my day, rather than my day running me, I'm able to start all of our day on the right foot. There are so many times when things don't go as planned during the morning hours getting ready for our day. By creating margin first thing in the morning I have created the extra allowance of bandwidth necessary to handle whatever comes my way.

Morning margin, as I like to call it, is a powerful tool because it serves as a catalyst for the rest of the day. If I spend time with God first thing in the morning in prayer and meditation I'm far more likely to have increased patience and a sense of purpose during the day. When I work out first thing in the morning, I tend to make better nutritional choices at breakfast, lunch, and dinner. Just waking up early provides a sense of pride and accomplishment, and all I did was open my eyes and force myself out of bed! If you haven't established a morning routine yet and want to make a big change in your life, just wake up fifteen minutes earlier tomorrow. Do this every day for the next week, and then do the same the following week. If you have trouble not hitting the snooze button, set your phone somewhere away from the bed so you have to physically get up to turn off the alarm. Or spend $15 on Amazon and buy an almost extinct item called an alarm clock! Start with something as simple as writing down one thing you're grateful for each day and progress to reading something that will improve your life. I once had a mentor tell me if I read a proverb from the Bible every day for a year I would have more wisdom than 99 percent of the people around me. If you're not a Christian or a Bible person, that's perfectly ok, and this still applies to you. The person who wrote Proverbs was King Solomon, and he's regarded as the wisest and wealthiest individual of all time. Regardless of your religious background, why would you not want to learn from the wisest and wealthiest person ever? There are also thirty-one Proverbs, so it's as if they were designed to read one a day, and you can finish the entire book in a month. It's hard to explain, but I can tell you firsthand that nothing has impacted my life more than getting up early in the morning and reading a Proverb a day.

Now you might not have a home gym, but everybody's got a pair of running shoes, or you can YouTube exercise videos and do them in your living room. Again, feelings follow behaviors, so it's just a matter of getting after it and the rest will follow. I have found that when I go to the gym there's a lot of distractions, so I created a workout area at home. I want to get in and get out and move on with my day, but do whatever works for you so you can create morning margin and set up a routine to give yourself allowance to better handle the stress of your day. If you're not already exercising in the morning, then begin by stretching or going for a walk. Listen to podcasts during your exercise time focused on topics of interest to you. The key isn't how much you do as much as it is the consistency with which you do it.

By establishing morning margin in your life, you will begin to see how it leads to the establishment of other positive habits. For example, since I'm early to rise, I have to go to bed early. Therefore we don't watch much if any TV in the evenings and only have televisions in entertainment areas of our home. In fact, we cut cable over a decade ago and started Heather's business as a result! If you have a TV in your bedroom, I recommend you remove it immediately. When Heather and I went through premarital counseling over fourteen years ago, our counselor told us the bedroom is for three things: sleeping, communicating, and having sex...and TV is not one of the three. We took his word for it and over a decade later our marriage is much better off thanks to his sage advice. The new challenge we face is the use of mobile phones in the bedroom. Heather and I have made it a pact that we will put up our phones when we walk into the bedroom and place them on chargers away from the bed. The discipline to not have a TV in the bedroom or use our cellphones in bed is all driven by the morning margin principle and it's been a game changer for our marriage and family.

THE BIG MO

Last year we had a day of snowfall in Charleston that accumulated over five inches of snow. This is highly unusual for Charleston, and as you can imagine, everyone freaked out. School was cancelled for several days and everyone took to the streets to find the biggest hill we could find to do some sledding. Keep in mind people from the south don't have shovels or sleds, so you saw people sledding on the most hilarious objects. I sent our kids down the hill on a giant peacock pool inflatable! After sledding, we made our way back home to build a giant snowman, and the snow was perfect packing density. We started with a small snowball, and after rolling it around the yard a few times, we had created a giant mass of snow that would become the base for our snowman. What I learned about life through building a snowman is momentum matters. When you start small by waking up fifteen minutes earlier or begin practicing gratitude each morning, it's like the tiny snowball before it gets rolling. However, after you've successfully gotten up early for a period of time and implemented morning margin, the "Big MOmentum" will begin to carry you forward.

Creating momentum in your life through daily habits will set you on the path towards peak performance. When I bring up the words peak performance you might immediately think of a professional or Olympic athlete. Why do we relegate peak performance to certain areas of life but not others? Have you ever considered achieving peak performance as a father? Achieving peak performance in anything is about sustained performance over time. Attaining peak performance as a dad is no different, and there are many factors to focus on like spiritual, mental, physical, emotional, financial, social, and career. Why do we not focus on peak performance as a dad the way a professional athlete hones their game or the disciplined focus we apply to our work? Is it not more important to have the concept of peak performance as a dad? Too often in life we try to attain high levels of performance in areas that don't matter or are inconsequential in the grand scope of life. Certainly, business and sports achievements matter, but I want my dad achievements to outshine them all. In order to get there, you have to look at your life and say, "Am I striving for peak performance in every area?" Look at your current status in each area as a dad and no matter where you are, put a plan in place to move forward. You climb a mountain by taking the first step and as fathers we can ascend the summit together.

LEARNING TO SAY NO

Time is your most valuable asset, and making the best use of your time helps you create margin, but we waste so much time in the day, much of it because we have a hard time saying no. At times I have a challenge in my life with saying no to things outside of my family because of all the career, social, and philanthropic demands. Our schedule can so easily get crammed with things that don't matter and that we, frankly, don't want to do. The hardest promise to keep is the one that you don't want to. That creates a schedule with no margin and no allowance, and that's where things spiral out of control.

Andy Stanley, the founder of North Point Ministries, says, "You have to trust that what you don't do will multiply what you do do." I love that quote because if we can become masters at saying no, it will allow us to focus on doing the right things right. That's such an important concept for us as fathers to grasp because every one of those "no's" brings us closer to our best "yes." I've never regretted telling a buddy no or missing a business meeting in return for watching my kid's game, attending a school performance, or surprising them for lunch. My best "yes" is my family, end of story.

If it's not on my calendar, it's not happening! This is a best practice I've put in place in order to guard my time and ensure I'm delivering on my promises. Calendaring everything helps me create margin. I found that if I don't put it on my calendar it won't happen. I can also be really protective of my time because when you time block it on the calendar, I don't care if it's digital or on paper, the practice of calendaring allows you to create your best day and your best week. I also don't have separate calendars for work and life, either, because I don't want to isolate those two areas of my life. That's like being married and having separate checking accounts, which just doesn't make sense to me. By combining work and life calendars, my coworkers can see when I'm busy with my family, like the one day a week I'm joining my kids for lunch at school. If it's on my calendar, it's blocked off. That time is sacred; it's preserved. And how cool is it when somebody at work looks into my calendar and sees these events that revolve around my family or role as a parent?

I do daddy-daughter date nights once a month, and if I don't put that on my calendar then it won't happen. Caution! If you have a daughter and you do date nights, ensure you at minimum double up on the amount of dates you take your wife on. While Heather thinks it's adorable that Hayden and I have our date nights, I can assure you she would not be happy if I didn't recipro-cate with date nights for her. It was also really fun when Hayden was younger to say, "Hey Hayden, what's your calendar look like this month for daddy-daughter date night?" And she gets out her little play calendar, which is wide open, of course, yet she'd act like her schedule was full and she had to "fit me in!" Do you know how important that made her feel to know she was a priority of mine? My boys not so much. They just say, "Dad, we don't need to look. We're wide open." But they sure liked it when I made the commitment to coach flag football for them this year. It was a commitment of at least two days a week in the evenings, typically Tuesdays and Thurs-days, and I put it on my calendar and blocked that time off. I knew—and others knew—that I had to leave work early for about a month and a half, two days a week to make that happen. I was able to create the margin to do that even as a busy executive with an insane schedule because I was intentional about it. You need to make fatherhood as much a part of your day as business meetings. You have to be as intentional with fatherhood as you are with work life and social life and make it part of your daily schedule or else it won't happen. Try this for thirty days, and I guarantee your schedule will become filled with what matters most and you will de-prioritize what matters least.

A HIGHER CALLING

I look at the story in the Bible when Nehemiah was rebuilding Jerusalem. He was building this massive wall, leading this big team, but there were people who were trying to oppose the rebuilding of the wall, asking Nehemiah to stop the work.

"Look," he told them, "I'm doing a great work, and I can't come down."

We have to approach parenting with that level of velocity where we literally say, "Look, I'm doing a great work, and I cannot come down." That mindset has helped so much when I have those competing interests or competing time on my calendar because I'm able to say no. I'm not willing to go to my daughter and say, "Hey, sweetheart, we've got to push off date night because I have to take on this project at work." You do that one time, and it's just going to happen again and again. It's never easy to tell someone no, but the more you do it, the easier it gets. Now, I'm not saying you have to be so staunch about it that it's like, "No, no, no, no; the only thing I do is be a parent." That's not what I'm saying here, but with all the other things pulling at you, it's vital that you learn to say no to almost anything that isn't essential. It all goes back to setting yourself up for success. You can either run your day or your day can run you.

I've taken a viewpoint in my life where I'll have plenty of time to socialize, play golf, watch sports, whatever, when my kids have either left the home or are older and are kind of doing their own thing, but right now, I make them a priority in my life. I'm doing a great work right now as a dad, and I can't come down, so that requires some sacrifices on my part. My social life has certainly suffered, and I'm a social being. I love being around people. I love entertaining, so I've tried to create social opportunities that include other families with children or other dads and their kids. If there's a big Clemson football game I want to watch, we host at our house or go to somebody else's house so all the kids can play while the dads are watching the game, and we're all having a great time. You don't have to eliminate everything from your life just because you're a father, it just takes a little thought about how to blend the two together.

When you can combine the two, then you have the best of both worlds. Sometimes you just have to be creative. Maybe your son doesn't play golf, but he loves driving the cart and hunting for golf balls in the woods. They just want to be included in what you're doing and enjoy seeing you with your friends, which is a valuable experience in and of itself. Or perhaps you can take one of them on a business trip, like Rusty Shelton from Texas has done with his son. He even got him his own little sports jacket. Rusty's a great speaker, so his son has seen him speak on stage. The value of your kid seeing you interact in that environment or speaking to a group is huge.

The best part is when you do say yes to things that don't include your children, you won't feel tension because you've made them a priority again and again. When you do say yes to go play golf, it's because you're getting to go play at Augusta National, not the local country club. In 2017, I attended the College Football National Championship with my friends Stewart Killgallon and Vincent Jackson in Tampa, Florida, to watch my Clemson Tigers win on the last play. My kids were so excited for me as it was a once in a lifetime opportunity. It's so meaningful that your kids are excited for you. You're fully present and fully engaged in the event. You don't have the opposite tension of feeling like you should be at home with your wife and children because you've already put them first by making deposits of time again and again. If you do this right, margin gives you freedom—freedom to be engaged and fully present in whatever you're doing—and it allows you to appropriately manage the tension in life so that whether you're with your kids or you're engaged in something else, you're fully there and you don't have the baggage of feeling like you could be or should be somewhere else. If you make those small investments with your kids, it allows you make those big withdrawals when you need to make it, like for a big sporting event or guys' weekend.

One thing I enjoy most about leading this movement is all of the stories I receive from other fathers who are implementing the principles of Daddy Saturday and seeing the positive results in their marriages and children's lives. Nick Read is one of the fathers who has really bought into the Daddy Saturday movement and shared his story with me. Nick started intentionally taking his daughter out of the house for a couple of hours on Saturdays so his wife could do whatever she wanted to do. He takes his daughter to get a manicure, have breakfast, or play in the park, and it's really brought them closer together, while giving his wife a break to exercise, shop, or do what's meaningful to her. He's been intentional with his time and his calendar, and the benefit and the blessing hasn't only been for him and his daughter—it's also been for his wife, as well. The only problem is that now when they sit down to watch TV together as a family in the evenings, his daughter jumps up on his lap and not hers, so she's like, "Hey, what the heck's going on?" When I heard this story I gave him a big fist bump and said, "Welcome to Daddy Saturday."

Just like Nick in the story above, you can begin to make small investments in the life of your child, and if you do this often enough when they are young, the deposits you make will pay dividends when they grow up. It's natural as your kids grow up they will want to spend more time hanging out with their friends and possibly less time with you. I know it hurts, but it's true! I'm already experiencing this with Hayden Olivia as she's now eleven and has a full schedule with hip-hop dancing, volleyball, and cheerleading. She's not involved in every Daddy Saturday, and you know what, that's ok. She still spends more time with me than a typical preenager would. I attribute this to all the deposits I've made over her first ten-plus years of life, the traditions and the consistency in our communication. I also believe she experiences "FOMO" or the Fear Of Missing Out when she's not a part of Daddy Saturday. When provided with a choice, she more often than not chooses to spend the day with us because it's fun and she looks forward to it. She's protective of our time together because it's meaningful to her, and your kids will be too.

THE SPARTAN WAY

It was around 6:30 a.m. on a late January morning and I had just finished my morning workout. Heather came running out of the house upon hearing me scream several times in a high-pitched tone. Once she saw what I was up to she simply shook her head, said "you're crazy!" and proceeded to get me a towel. I had decided to make a polar bear plunge part of my morning routine. The water temperature was sub-sixty degrees and took my breath away as I slowly walked into the icy pool water, hence my screaming. There is no other way to say it, getting into cold water always sucks! My goal is to stay in for at least one minute and eventually three minutes. After a few times of walking into the icy water, I began getting comfortable with being uncomfortable.

Another way of creating margin is with the concept of getting comfortable with being uncomfortable. There are many uncomfortable situations as a dad you have to put yourself into. It can be uncomfortable going against the culture of the world and what's trendy. It can be uncomfortable disciplining your child instead of doing what's comfortable and trying to be their friend. Just because everybody else is tethered to their phones and putting in fifty- or sixty-hour work weeks doesn't mean you have to, too. But if you train yourself to be comfortable with being uncomfortable, you can swim against the tide. I put myself in uncomfortable situations routinely so that when I have to engage in an uncomfortable situation, I'm able to respond naturally and work through it more easily.

One of things I've started doing this year, for instance, is Spartan Races, which are obstacle course races. I've ran farther, pushed myself harder, and done more physically than I ever thought I could do, and I'm a very active person. The training just to be able to do the races is very uncomfortable in and of itself, while the race is extremely uncomfortable. Spartan participants run from three to fourteen miles and encounter from twenty to thirty-five obstacles, like overhead ladders, rock-climbing walls, and barbed wire fencing you have to crawl under in thick mud. The best part is the finish line, which is a pile of burning logs you get to jump over. After running fourteen miles, overcoming thirty-five obstacles, and jumping over fire, I feel so much more comfortable when I encounter something that's uncomfortable in life, like saying no at work, managing work-life tension, or just having to push through something I don't want to.

If you don't want to sign up for a Spartan Race, just start flossing your teeth every night. Now that might not sound like a big deal to you, but it is to me because I really hate it. About a year and a half ago, my dentist asked me if I was flossing.

"No," I responded. "I use mouthwash in place of floss."

He laughed and said, "Well, I know you're a 110 percent kind of guy, but did you know that by not flossing you're only covering about 35 percent of your teeth. You're missing the other 65 percent."

He let that sink in for a minute before adding, "So, Justin, are you a 110 percent kind of guy or are you a 35 percent kind of guy?"

I was just like, "Oh my gosh, you got me."

He knew the exact button to push to trigger me and it worked. I've flossed every single night for over a year now and not only has my oral health improved, but so has my willpower because that's the last thing I feel like doing at the end of a long day. I force myself to do it, but here's the weirdest thing: when I finish, it's like there's a tiny surge of dopamine because I'm doing something I didn't want to do at the point of the day when I didn't want to do it the most. It actually makes it easier to get up early the next morning because I flossed my teeth the night before and got that little surge of reward for doing something I didn't want to do. As crazy as it sounds, flossing has become a margin-creating habit in my life and impacts so many other things, so I need to give my dentist a huge thank you.

We are the sum of every choice that we make. Our choices

make us. That's the power of saying no to the wrong things and yes to the right things. Every one of those little choices builds margin and adds up to making us who we are as a parent in the life of our kids. Are we going to be the father who said yes to engaging our kids, or the one who said yes to things that don't really matter? The choice is yours.

BONUS MATERIAL

Creating margin has been a game changer and radically improved my life in so many ways. Want tips and tools for how to gain more margin in your life? Go to our bonus site for videos and free tips and tools available for download. Go to www.DaddySaturday.com/bonus

CHAPTER FOUR

STOP TRYING TO BE A HERO

"The most important thing in life is to just be yourself. Unless you can be Batman. Always be Batman."

—UNKNOWN

Pretty much every movie that's ever been made follows a familiar pattern: there's a hero, there's a villain, and there's some sort of conflict that occurs with the hero typically emerging victorious. But also amidst the conflict, you have a guide who leads the hero to success or helps that hero recover from failure. Look at the first *Star Wars* film: Luke Skywalker is the hero and Darth Vader is the villain. There's the conflict of darkness versus light, and you've got Yoda, the little green guy, who emerges as the guide to help Luke Skywalker along the journey.

Too often, as fathers, we try to make ourselves the hero of the story; we try to live our lives through our children and, unintentionally or not, play the role of hero for egotistical reasons or as a means of overcoming our own insecurities. I'm sure you've seen that "Dad is my Hero" T-shirt, but that's actually the completely wrong approach, because if the dad is the hero of the story, then it positions the child to never experience failure or achieve success on his or her own. You get a generation that emerges much like Gen Y or Millennials (those born between 1981–1996), often called the "Snowflake Generation." Whether true or not, older generations perceive them as being less psychologically resilient or more emotionally vulnerable, so Gen Y didn't have the opportunity to experience failure as children, making them more fragile as adults. It's a generation where everyone got a trophy for participation. When everyone succeeds, no one fails. This was never more evident than on the hugely popular talent show *American Idol*. People who thought they were superstar performers would audition only to find out that they're terrible, but no one ever told them that. In fact, they were probably told the opposite: "You can do and be anything you want to be!" so it's not their fault. They're the product of the society that they grew up in, and in many cases, it's because their dad positioned himself as the hero of the story.

I was born in 1981, so I'm at the very start of the Millennial generation, but I relate much more to the previous generation, Gen X, purely because of how I was raised. I have a bit of an old-soul mentality if you haven't figured that out already. I've worked in environments mostly made up of Millennials, so much of my experience and my commentary is from what I see every day in my social and work environments with Millennials, and how they experience success and failure. I'm also seeing and experiencing firsthand how they parent, which they're just starting to do. There's this humongous opportunity with Millennials to really change the dynamic of parenthood. However, that's not going to be an easy task based on the way Millennials were raised. If you are a Millennial parent reading this, you need to know you have the potential to be the greatest generation of parents ever in this country. You are also a vital generation for fatherhood because Gen Z is right behind you watching your every move. If we are going to be successful as parents and change the future generations, it's imperative Millennial parents understand their potential and the possible pitfalls based on how they were raised. The most pressing pitfall I see in Millennial parents today is failing to "future proof" by not allowing a child to overcome their fear or experience failure. If Millennial parents can set aside their upbringing and realize fear of failure is natural and failure as a child can be a good thing if handled appropriately, then they can absolutely become incredible role models for future parents and for their children. Let me be clear, I'm not saying Millennial parents are wrong in their parenting style, I'm simply saying there's a better way that can produce the outcomes in children to create world changers.

In addition to parenting, I've also found this hero-less mindset also works as a manager, especially with the Millennial generation. Many times I would be in my office, and there would be a knock on the door. It's the, "Hey, got a second?" moment, which to me means this person has a monkey on their back. I imagine this monkey literally clinging to their back, and it's about to jump off their back and onto mine, and then they're going to walk out of the office and leave the monkey with me. By the end of the day, I have a barrel of monkeys in my office, and I'm like, *How did that happen to me?* Now, I make the individual take their monkeys back with them. I literally had a barrel of monkeys sitting on my desk and monkeys hanging from my ceiling as a reminder to my team. In order to give their monkey back I tell them when they come to me with a problem, they also need to bring at least two solutions they've thought of on their own. What I've found is I'm encouraging the individual to self-coach, and now they often self-solve the problem; they don't even come to me in the first place.

"Dad, [Insert Kid's Name] isn't playing fair and keeps making up their own rules to the game!" If I had dollar for every time one of my kids came to me with something like this I would be a rich man. I think the same thing happens a lot—your kids come to you with a problem and, as a parent, you want to be the hero and just immediately provide the solution. Let's face it, providing the solution is far easier in the moment than it is to have that dialogue or that conversation to help them work through it. When my children come to me with a problem, my default now is to say, "Okay, well, have you thought about what we could do to fix or change that?" Even at an early age, they're starting to learn to self-coach because I'm putting the accountability back on them.

In the process, I'm making them the hero of their own story, not me.

THE GUIDE TO BEING A GUIDE

Millennial parents have a tremendous opportunity to flip the paradigm in their parenting to take up this role of being a guide rather than a hero, but it's going to be hard for them to do because of how they were raised. Many Millennials had a hero parent in their life, so they're going to have to fight against the paternal example instilled in them. It's vital all parents, but especially Millennial parents, realize how important it is that their children experience failure along with success and that as fathers they serve as the guide not the hero. As fathers we shouldn't paint failure as a negative outcome because

I would much rather let my kids fail when they're eight than when they're twenty-eight. Failure for an eight-year-old is, I ran with the ice cream cone in my hand, the ice cream fell off the top, and I no longer have an ice cream cone. Failure at eighteen or twenty-eight is, I lost my job because of underperformance and have now entered a downward spiral of depression, drinking, drugs, and potentially suicide because I've never experienced failure before. You can see this currently playing out with the Millennial generation as adults. For many, adulthood is the first time they've ever experienced failure and most don't know how to process the experience. By not having the prior experience of working through failure and building some internal grit, failure has the potential to become a catastrophic event in their life. Failure is not only much larger when you get older, but the ability to handle failure later in life is much more difficult if you haven't experienced it earlier on, and it can have far-reaching repercussions. Failure is part of life. If you're not experiencing failure in life, then you're not living life. Successful people are typically standing on a mountain of failure. As hard as it may be, letting your children experience failure now has the opportunity to set them up for success later in life.

Sports can be a great way to teach your kids about failure and success. I was coaching my son Blane in flag football when he was eight years old. Blane's team was still at the level where they're not playing full-on games, so success or failure still really didn't completely count, which makes sense for recreation sports at an early age. But Blane knew the situation: His team was down by a score. There was one play left, and playing quarterback, the ballgame was in his hands. If he scored a touchdown, his team would win the game; if he didn't score, he would let his team down and experience failure. I walked over to him in the huddle and reiterated some wise advice that had once been told to me.

"Hey, Blane," I said. "No matter what happens, whether you score and win the game or whether you don't and we don't win, we're still getting ice cream after the game."

He looked at me, and it was like all the pressure drained from his face. He knew that the success or failure of the game was in his hands, but there was no pressure from anybody else on the outside, and the outcome was completely up to him. If he scored and they won the game, great; if he didn't, he'd move on, he'd learn from it, and we'd still go get ice cream. We were both fine with whatever the outcome was. I wasn't trying to live through him. I was just supporting him as a guide and showing him that you're going to have success, you're going to have failure. He ended up not scoring and was stopped just short of the goal line, so he didn't end up winning the game for his team, but we still got ice cream and our relationship didn't change a bit. I fulfilled the role as the guide instead of trying to be the hero and telling him exactly what to do and how he needed to run the play. I left the outcome up to him and he owned it. Most importantly, I preserved our relationship and allowed him to be a kid. I know the next time he gets in that circumstance, he's going to be even more equipped to have success. The guide is there to help your kids see, if they have success, then what did they do that lead to the success? If they experienced failure, then how do they learn from it and move forward? As dads we need to be more like Yoda and less like Luke Skywalker.

EARNED NOT GIVEN

In most recreation leagues there are still trophies or medals everyone gets for participation in a sport where a score isn't officially kept. In the club leagues or the more advanced sport programs it's all about winning or losing. Awards in these leagues are based on performance and outcomes. My daughter, Hayden, does competitive hip hop, and they don't get trophies unless they perform and place in the competition. There's no trophy just for being on the team. I like to do Spartan Races, as I mentioned previously, and my kids do a Spartan Kids Race. And while they all get a medal for finishing, the back of the medal says, "Earned not given." While racing they have to climb slippery muddy walls, carry heavy wet sandbags, and overcome obstacles that many times they can't conquer on their first attempt. They have to cross the finish line after overcoming all of the obstacles in order to get a medal, so I am choosing to put my kids in situations where they get the experience of having to train, prepare, and earn a reward dependent on the outcome. It's not just something given to them. Seeing the smiles on my kids' faces when they cross the finish line in a Spartan Kids Race is one of the proudest moments I've had as a father. My kids have never worn a participation medal to school the next day, but you can be sure they had all three of their Spartan Kids Trifecta medals around their neck and were "dripping" in the success of their accomplishment.

I can remember when I was in Little League baseball at age nine and was on an all-star team that ended up getting third place in a tournament. We all gathered for the team photo afterward with our third-place trophies, and I was furious. I was the catcher, so I still had my shin guards on, and I vividly recall after the photo was taken, breaking that trophy over my knee. I was so upset because we had gotten third place and didn't win the whole tournament. I was upset with not performing at my best. I was only nine, but I had that mentality of wanting to win and to compete to be the best.

My life was built on this concept of knowing if I worked hard and listened to those around me—my coaches, my teachers, my parents—and drew wisdom from them, it would lead to success on the field or in the classroom. Much of my life has been built on the momentum of those wins, those successes, but there have also been plenty of failures along the way. When I was younger, I had this habit of doing what I called sandbagging. I was so competitively driven that if I didn't win or knew I wasn't going to, I had this tendency to sandbag it, to throw in the towel, and it would take me awhile to recover. But I started to learn that the faster I could shift my mindset and recover from that, the better my performance would be. Interestingly, I've already seen the same behaviors in my son Blane, even at a young age, where if something doesn't come easily to him, if he doesn't have success right away and it gets hard, he has the same tendency to sandbag it. One of the most challenging things about being a parent can be parenting the YOU out of your child!

We live on the coast of South Carolina, so we have the great opportunity to take advantage of the beach and the ocean really any time we want. Blane came to me one day and said he wanted to take up surfing, so I said I'd go "halfsies" with him on a board. He saved up his money, and one day he got his board. I have some friends who are surfers, and asked him if he wanted a lesson from one of them.

"No, Dad," he said. "I just want to go and try it. I can do this."

All right, I thought, *he's a natural athlete, let him give it a try.* We set off one beautiful summer morning with a good swell coming in. Not surprisingly, Blane got up on the board pretty quickly without any tips from me, but then the waves started to get bigger, and he started falling off the board. I could literally see his mindset shift in his head from, *This is fun, I've got this!* to *I can't do this, the waves are too big, I'm going to fall,* and he proceeded to fall off the next five waves before even catching them. I finally waded out and grabbed the board.

"Hey, Blane," I said. "I can see doubt in your eyes, and it's causing you to fall off the board before the wave even gets to you. As you catch it, tell yourself, 'I'm going to catch this wave and surf it all the way in. I've got this!'"

He muttered "okay" under his breath, and I said, "No, Blane, I want you to say that out loud as you start to ride the wave."

The next wave came, he stood up on the board, shouted that out and rode the wave the entire way. It was really just a mindset shift of saying, *I can do this!* I didn't tell him how to do it. He did that all himself. I was just there to inspire him and serve as a guide. He was the hero of his own story. But just like in the movies, it's hard to be the hero if you don't experience failure first. I'm there as the guide to help them learn from the failures and let them know that mindset and intention matter a great deal.

Why is this so important? Because like any parent I naturally want to save my children and be their hero. As a father I want to be the superhero that never lets them fall. However, since serving as guide rather than a hero, I'm seeing my kids beginning to problem solve for themselves, grow and learn from their failures, and gain a sense of self-reliance and grit that will allow them to succeed when life gets tough. It's so against the grain for me to step back and to serve as the guide because I desperately want to be my kids' hero. I want to step in and save the day when they're down or not experiencing success. But realize it's a short-term win and a long-term loss. You may be winning the game, but you're losing the overall battle of preparing your kids for life in the world.

THE MORE GUIDES THE BETTER

One of the most freeing things about being a guide and not the hero is that it allows me to seek out other guides I can help surround my kids with in areas that aren't my strengths. I am the least handy person in the world. I'm like Chip Gaines in our family and Heather is our Joanna Gaines. DEMO DAY! is my favorite and I have an elementary ability to do anything handy. Construction, auto mechanics, and things like that are just not in my wheelhouse because I was taught how to throw a curveball and a spiral growing up. I wasn't taught how to work on a car or build things. If I'm trying to be the hero at everything for my kids and don't ever show vulnerability in areas where I'm weak, then my kids won't have the opportunity to discover and develop if it's an area of gifting for them. If I'm playing hero of all things as a dad, I'm going to have a hard time releasing authority to another man who could help my kids develop in an area I'm not educated or talented in. As a guide, I'm constantly surrounding my kids with a team of talented men who help them discover and grow in their areas of passion and talent. I'm sure you don't have this problem, but my kids tend to listen to other people rather than their parents so this becomes a win-win as they are influenced more quickly and grow faster sometimes when it's not coming from Dad.

The earlier you can move into the position of a guide in your kids' lives, the better your long-term relationships with them will be. When your kids become teenagers, when they get into college, when they become newly married, when they become parents themselves, they don't need a hero. They're independent at that point. That's when they need a guide or a wise sage more than ever. When they bump up against those life experiences and need pure wisdom, if you've built that into the relationship from an early stage, it's naturally going to be there when they get older. And you're going to have a far greater chance of them reaching out to you as a guide when they need it the most. Dads, you are your kids' hero and you always will be, so stop trying to be one and instead assume your rightful place as their guide.

BONUS MATERIAL

Visit www.DaddySaturday.com/bonus for a video on how to be a GUIDE and allow your kids to be the HERO.

CHAPTER FIVE

FAR MORE IS CAUGHT THAN TAUGHT

"Attitudes are caught, not taught."

—MR. FRED ROGERS

Have you ever heard the phrase, "Sun's out, guns out"? The boys in our household never seem to be wearing clothes, especially their shirt...yes, I'm the ringleader here. One day we were all sitting around the table with our shirts off, and I was giving the boys compliments about how "swoll" they were getting (note: "swoll" for an eight-, six-, and four-year-old is like a small golf ball in their bicep.) I flexed my muscles and said the now famous line in our home, "Sun's out, guns out!" and proceeded to kiss both of my biceps, one at a time. My boys laughed and I walked away not thinking anything of it. About a week later one of our neighbors called me and said our six-year-old, Mason, was playing at their house with his shirt off and proceeded to kiss both of his biceps and say, "Sun's out, guns out!" She was dying laughing and just had to let me know about Mason's muscles.

As fathers, we must be mindful of how we behave around our children, because they will pick up far more of what they see than what they hear. About a year ago, I was fortunate to spend over an hour with former Ford CEO Alan Mulally. We were discussing business and we got on the topic of parenting and he shared something with me I will never forget. He said, "The biggest problem with communication is the illusion that it occurs." How true is that statement not only in life and business, but with our children! The average person needs to hear something seven times to truly take it in, and with kids it can be even more. Yet, one instance of watching you engage in a certain behavior can become instantly ingrained in their memory banks.

I had a mentor, Michael "Dee" Dowis, who demonstrated the concept of caught vs taught better than anyone I've ever been around. I met Dee when he hired me for my first real job out of Clemson as a drug representative. Dee played quarterback for the Air Force and set many NCAA records and even beat out Emmitt Smith in the Heisman voting his senior year. Dee was an incredibly talented athlete, but he was also one of the most humble people you could ever meet. One day we were talking to this guy who was a walk-on at a not-to-be-named SEC school and he was bragging about his glory days. He was gloating about how good he was and regaling Dee and me with his football stories. I endured his ranting because I was waiting for Dee to put him in his place with his stories of records and Heisman votes. Instead, Dee just let him talk and politely excused us from the conversation. I was like, "Dee, what's wrong with you—why didn't you let that cocky benchwarmer have it?" He replied, "I have nothing to prove to him and clearly he had a lot to prove to us!" I will never forget the lesson I learned on what humility looks like that day, and I've tried to pass along many lessons like this I caught from Dee to my children. Unfortunately, I lost my friend and mentor as Dee passed away in a tragic car accident. When I look back at my time with Dee, it's not the many things he taught me that I remember, it's the values and principles I caught by watching him. His legacy lives on through his wife and children, the many people he impacted, and certainly through me and the similar impact I hope to have on my children.

If you are like me then you have expectations on how your kids should behave. You expect them to catch the right things and listen when you teach them. However, have you ever considered the same behaviors we don't want to see in our kids are the very behaviors we model the most? We don't want our kids to lose their temper, yet if they see us getting upset over little things and losing our temper, chances are they're going to react the same way. I find it ironic that we'll get upset at our children for getting angry over something small, and yet, we might be doing the very thing that we're trying to discourage them from doing, and in my experience children tend to pick up on negative behaviors more easily than positive behaviors. As Rabbi Noach Orlowek says, "We are not raising moral children. We are raising children to become moral adults." That's one of my guideposts; we must choose the behaviors we want our kids to model, and let them see you as a father modeling the cornerstone daily habits of diet and exercise, the use of digital devices, finances, and core character traits in a positive way. If fathers do this right, we have the potential to change the trajectory of our children's lives, and once caught, they will not depart from it.

MODEL BEHAVIOR

I discovered I had food allergies later in life, and it's caused me to have a restrictive diet. I avoid gluten, dairy, soy, and a variety of other foods that basically represent all of the fun food groups. Breakfast is typically the most difficult meal for me, so I often make smoothies. Mason is my most observant child and he watches my every move. I noticed him checking out my smoothies in the morning and he began asking me questions about why I never have pancakes and what I like to put in my smoothies. Eventually, he asked if he could have a smoothie of his own and I hooked him up with an almond milk, frozen blueberry, banana, and frozen spinach smoothie! Not a bad breakfast for a six-year-old, and it's become an incredible way to hide all sorts of green things in his diet. Guess what happened next? The rest of my kids also started asking for smoothies in the morning. They don't have smoothies every day, and they certainly get their share of chocolate chip pancakes and donuts from the grandparents, but overall I was able to shape my kids' diets by allowing them to catch the positive behavior from my diet.

It's imperative as fathers we begin allowing our children to catch us in the act of a healthy diet. The largest social experiment in the history of the human world is currently taking place. Outside of fatherlessness, childhood diabetes and the digital dilemma are the two biggest issues we must solve to save the next generation. In the U.S., the percentage of children and adolescents affected by obesity has more than tripled since the 1970s. Data from 2015–2016 show that nearly one in five school-age children and young adults (6–19 years old) in the U.S. has obesity.[3] Let me be blunt: this is unacceptable! If you look at the rate of childhood obesity and the overall health of

---

3 Centers for Disease Control and Prevention, "Childhood Obesity Facts," *CDC 24/7*, January 29, 2018, https://www.cdc.gov/healthyschools/obesity/facts.htm.

our children, it starts with the example we're setting for them in our microwavable, fast-food, couch-potato society. As fathers we must model the behaviors we desire in our children if we are going to change the next generation and solve the diabetes dilemma.

Imagine the following two scenarios and tell me which one has the better chance of establishing a healthy child who grows into a healthy adult.

Scenario 1: After a long day of work, a dad comes home, sits down to a dinner of processed food, and then proceeds to watch television for a couple of hours while cracking open a few beers.

Scenario 2: After exercising early in the morning and a long day of work, a dad comes home, sits down to a healthy dinner of organic foods, reads books with his children and independently for a few hours while drinking water.

Your kids will catch the behaviors you most often engage in, and diet and exercise are two of the most important behaviors they will model after you.

You may think I'm being a bit dogmatic on the point of diet and exercise, but I can't argue with the positive results I've seen in my own life and in the lives of my family. Growing up we didn't have soda or artificial baked goods in house. To this day I've still never had a cavity (thanks Mom!). When Heather took our kids in for their annual checkups last year, one of the assistants in the pediatrician's office said, "Wow we haven't seen any of your kids this year. What a healthy family!" We've cut out 95 percent of the processed foods, shop almost exclusively at Whole Paycheck...I mean Whole Foods, and have removed artificial colorings from our children's diet. Studies have proven the negative effect of artificial colorings on children's mood and behavior, specifically some of the red, yellow, and blue dyes that are in many foods.[4] I've done my own double blind, placebo controlled anecdotal study and confirmed a notable change in my boys' behavior when they have red dye. If they have a large amount of red dye, they are especially hyperactive, rambunctious, and defiant, so we've chosen to cut them out. Unfortunately, so many foods contain dyes to make them look better and be more appealing. If you look at Doritos or Cheetos or any of the major chip brands, most of those have red dyes in them. Most soft drinks and sports drinks are also colored with dyes. Same with most hard candy that has a deep color like Skittles or Jolly Ranchers. They're also in barbecue sauce, fruit bars, and frosting. Pediatric studies have found that kids with ADHD in particular are adversely affected by arti-

---

4   Rachel Hennessey, "Living in Color: The Potential Dangers of Artificial Dyes,"
     Forbes, August 27 2012, https://www.forbes.com/sites/rachelhennessey/2012/08/27/
     living-in-color-the-potential-dangers-of-artificial-dyes/#462ac75a107a.

ficial food dyes.[5] No wonder some countries ban them! Clearly, mass market food companies care more about their profits than our children, and their lobbies are influencing government policy. As fathers, we need to set the example for our children, and while it's not convenient or inexpensive, it's vital to our children's future.

Never in the history of the world has so much food been available so cheaply and so easily. According to the Centers for Disease Control, which just released its latest findings on weight gain among adults in the U.S. from 1999–2016, the average male now weighs 197.9 pounds compared to 189.4, 20 years ago.[6] The average female weight has gone from 163.8 to 170.6, while the average waistline has expanded from 38.8 to 40.3, and 36.3 to 38.7, respectively. A major retailer also stated they've changed the way they size men's suits so as to not make people feel bad about the fact they were putting on so much weight. In other words, a suit that was a 44 or 46 twenty years ago is now labeled as a 42! We're living our lives out of convenience now, and we're teaching our kids the same thing. As a father, you've got to say, "Am I going to go the way the rest of the culture is going and take the easy,

---

5   "American Academy of Pediatrics Says Some Common Food Additives May Pose Health Risks to Children," *American Academy of Pediatrics*, July 23, 2018, https://www.aap.org/en-us/about-the-aap/aap-press-room/Pages/AAP-Says-Some-Common-Food-Additives-May-Pose-Health-Risks-to-Children.aspx.

6   Centers for Disease Control and Prevention, "Adult Obesity Facts," *CDC 24/7*, August 13, 2018, https://www.cdc.gov/obesity/data/adult.html.

convenient way and achieve the unhealthy results? Or am I going to do it the right way and achieve healthy results?" When society goes left, go right.

In the fall of 2018, I took a trip to Vietnam to help a client and friend, Phuong Uyen Tran, launch her book and I learned more about the United States by being in Vietnam than I did about Vietnam. The first stop on my return flight was Chicago O'Hare, and it was tremendous culture shock. I immediately noticed how overweight Americans are and the difference in the types of food that were available. Just about all the food in Vietnam was fish and produce sold in open markets. Real, whole foods. When I came back to the U.S., I was amazed by how much processed and fast food there was and how convenient it was to eat, which I had taken for granted. In Southeast Asia, they have to work so hard just to have the basic necessities. In the U.S., we have access to so many things that make it very easy to engage in really bad habits, which then are passed on to our children. As dads we need to be diligent and take a vested interest in leading by example because the society we live in will not set the right example for us.

Today's children also have no concept of where real food comes from in our culture. I had a father write me from Utah to tell me about how he wanted to teach his children about where real food comes from, so he started a small herb and vegetable garden in their backyard, which the kids are responsible for. He talked about how his kids love planting the seeds and watching the plants grow. The actual food the garden produces is simply a by-product; what the children get to see is that there are things in life that take time. There are things in life you can't just order off Amazon. Well, I guess you can order vegetables off Amazon now that the company owns Whole Foods, but it's not the same as growing them. And how much more fun is that when you actually get to grow the produce, cultivate it, and then make it a part of your meal? The kids get such a sense of pride and accomplishment.

Breakfast may be the most nutritionally important meal, but I like to say family dinner is the most relationally important meal of the day. The breakdown of family dinners is driving a wedge in the relationships between fathers and their children. The velocity of our society and the mass of digital distractions has made gathering together for family dinner an exception rather than the rule. Dinnertime is where the magic happens for a family, is a centering point in the day, and is essential to maintaining a pulse on the family.

THE GREAT DIVIDE

The second biggest epidemic impacting our children is the digital dilemma. Let's face it, America is addicted to digital. There was a recent article written in *The New York Times* about a misperception of "the digital divide," where many were concerned with the fact that wealthier families and wealthier school districts have greater access to digital technology.[7] This would, in turn, give them an edge in terms of their education or careers. But, the article points out, what we're actually seeing is the contrary, where wealthier families are sharply limiting screen time, while poorer families are showing much more use of digital technology. We are now seeing far more promotion of iPads and computers in lower-income school districts than in higher-income school districts, including schools in the tech areas like Silicon Valley.

What does that tell you? These districts are going back to play-based activity in higher income areas, amounting to eight hours a day of screen time for lower-income children versus five-and-a-half hours a day for higher-income children. There's a divide all right, but it's the opposite of what you think. As people are now discovering, a lot of social media and other software is made to be addictive. That's how the software is engineered. Every time people hear a ding or feel a vibration informing them about a new text, email, or alert, it creates a surge of dopamine in the brain. Dopamine is the brain's pleasure-reward chem-

---

7   Nellie Bowles, "The Digital Gap Between Rich and Poor Kids is Not What We Expected," *The New York Times*, October 26, 2018, https://www.nytimes.com/2018/10/26/style/digital-divide-screens-schools.html.

ical, so when our children are using these apps, they're getting these surges of dopamine and it's causing them—and adults—to form a behavioral addiction.

We need to be really mindful of our own screen time, because if we want to encourage our children to appropriately use digital technology then we have to model it correctly. If we come home and we immediately are on our cell phone or tablet or we're on them first thing in morning in front of our children or watching excessive amounts of TV, then how can we expect our children not to do the exact same thing that we're modeling for them? Again, far more is caught than taught. If we want to break this digital addiction that is happening to our children and solve the digital dilemma, then we've got to model the behavior that we want to see in them.

If you were to ask a group of middle school students what they want to be when they grow up, at least half of them would say YouTube stars. Two of my four children will say the same at any given moment you ask them the question. My children absolutely engage in digital technology. We have a YouTube channel, Facebook page, Twitter handle, and Instagram channel for *Daddy Saturday*. We take advantage of and leverage social media and digital technology all the time, but we're doing it as creators and curators, not just as consumers, and that's the big difference. None of my kids have their own social media accounts, but they all help me as part of the Daddy Saturday social media crew. We've also spent time creating a business plan and allowing each of them to develop an online business to include a website and business collateral. Heather and I are working hard to ensure our children are making positive contributions to society as creators and not just consumers. Creating your own content, engaging with others, and learning to use the platforms for a potential business building tool or a branding tool are incredible skill sets for any child to possess. We are not only teaching our kids a skill they will be able to use later in life if they have the need, but also a mindset that it's important to be a more than just a consumer in anything you do.

Sure, there are certain times where we veg out and just watch funny videos on YouTube on our TV, but most of the time we're watching YouTube to get ideas for our next Daddy Saturday event, or we're watching it to gain content that we could use to engage others in our platform, so we're being productive. My two oldest boys love computers—they would be on the computer all day, every day if we let them—and we are working with the private Christian school they attend to allow them to engage in computer programming classes in the afternoon. We actually found the program and brought it to the school, so they can learn computer programming, which is a great use of screen time because it's the language of the future.

They're learning a language that's the backbone of everything we do in our society today and in the years to come.

OPEN THE BOOKS

Your children will most likely not learn anything about personal finance in school, so your ability to open the family books and allow them to observe your personal finances is another important behavior to model for your children. The amount of debt the Millennials and now Gen Z is acquiring, whether it's through student or consumer debt, is staggering.[8] It's another concerning issue in our society today, and the way we impact financial knowledge with our children is no different than the way you impact diet, health, and screen time—by engaging good financial principles and changing behavior. The first thing you have to do is create a budget, and include your children in budgeting conversations. It's kind of like open-book management for the family just as Jack Stack did in the corporate world with his book, *The Great Game of Business*. As the founder, president, and CEO of SRC Holdings Corporation in Missouri, he taught his employees how to treat business like a game thereby stripping away much of the complexity, so it made sense to everyone. Thanks to his management philosophy, SRC became

---

8   Megan Leonhardt, "Millennials Ages 25-34 Have $42,000 in Debt, and Most of it Isn't from Student Loans," CNBC.com, August 16, 2018, https://www.cnbc.com/2018/08/15/millennials-have-42000-in-debt.html.

one of the biggest turnaround stories of its time three decades ago.

Now my kids don't know everything that we make in terms of income, but we certainly let them see a lot of what the expenses are, so they start to understand the concept of money, how much it costs just to pay our mortgage, how much their private school costs. It helps to engage them in the right behavior at school, too, when they see the sacrifices we're making to send them to a private school. We also live in a society where they can press a button and buy something. There's no physical transaction, so the other thing we've tried to do is show them the flow of money. Before debit cards, we had to use cash at the grocery store and it stung a bit when you had to shell out $100, $150, or more. You feel that pain of flipping those 20s to pay for the groceries. Today, you insert a card in a machine and there's no physical reaction to spending money. It's invisible. Our kids don't see that either, so I often use cash for purchases just so they see how much something really costs.

Another component of personal finance we model for them is how to give and save. We've chosen to use Dave Ramsey's Financial Peace Junior methodology of 10 percent, 10 percent, 80 percent. When our kids make money, 10 percent goes as a tithe to the church and 10 percent goes to savings. The remaining 80 percent is theirs to spend, and Heather and I work to instill the principle of stewardship for the remaining 80 percent. Let me be clear: it's theirs to spend, we just help guide them to make good decisions with their money. If you are not familiar with the tithe, it's a biblical term that refers to bringing the first fruits of your labor back to God and the commandment is 10 percent. As Christians we believe it's all God's money anyway so he doesn't need our money. In fact, it's not that he wants something from us, it's that he wants something for us. As a family we've made the decision to tithe over 10 percent of our income back to the local church and we've involved our children in this practice. Whether you give to your local church or another worthy cause, the practice of generosity is something your kids will catch you doing and want to emulate in their own lives.

While we routinely give to our church, there's another principle called irrational or spontaneous generosity we do as a family. We often vote on giving opportunities, like helping a family in need around the holidays. In fact, it's become an important tradition for our family during the Christmas holiday. We give each of our children an envelope with 100 dollars—five $20 bills with each bill inside a Christmas card—$400 total, and we go out in the community, typically it's to the laundromat, the Waffle House, a homeless shelter, or halfway house. Each envelope has a little note on it that says Merry Christmas, and it's up to their discretion who gets it. We go to the laundromat because if somebody is doing laundry in a laundromat on Christmas Eve, they probably could use a little bit of hope and cheer at that moment. Same thing with the Waffle House. I cannot tell you some of the great memory burns we've had handing those envelopes out. It gives me chills just remembering the look on the people's faces when my children walk up to them, say "Merry Christmas," and hand them that envelope.

One memory I will never forget occurred three years ago in a Waffle House, where this older gentleman was sitting by himself. He was the only one in there, and my kids were a little nervous about approaching him. First, they gave the hostess, the waitress, and the cook envelopes, and then they walked over to this older gentleman. He looked up from his meal, and they handed him this silly looking penguin card that had this plastic bag on the inside of it with a $20 bill in it. The gentleman took it in his hands and held it like it was the most precious thing in the world. He just stared at that penguin as my children wished him a Merry Christmas. We walked outside toward the car bathed in the yellow glow of the Waffle House sign and turned around just in time to see him open the card. The biggest smile that I have ever seen crossed his face. To watch my kids watching him was priceless. We still talk about that man in the Waffle House every Christmas Eve and just how important the spirit of generosity and giving to others is. It's especially important knowing all the shiny plastic things that await them the next day.

Two years ago we went to a homeless shelter. We walked in the front entrance and told them what we were looking to do, and they said the family section was around the back. We had exactly seven envelopes left, and there were exactly seven families there. My kids walked around and gave each of those families a card. I could not believe the fact that there were seven families and we had seven cards left. I don't know what we would have done had there been eight families and came up one short! My kids will never forget that moment and neither will Heather and I, because the spirit of generosity is a lasting trait.

Last year we decided to fly to Ohio to visit my family on Christmas day. We saved several envelopes and decided to bless the airport workers and flight crew during our travels. We landed in Detroit, Michigan, and were walking from the gate to baggage claim and Mason had one card left. He had been holding it for a special person and was waiting for the right moment. He spotted a woman with a trash cart cleaning up the seating areas and he ran down the terminal to give her the card. I snapped a picture at just the right moment where he's extending the card into her hand, and every time I see that picture my heart melts into a puddle.

Since we started posting videos and photos of our generosity campaign, I've had many fathers send us messages of their ideas. A few notable ideas include working at the local soup kitchen, serving at a senior center, and paying for the person behind you in the drive through. My absolute favorite of all time came from a dad in New York who had his kids with him as they asked the homeless what they were in need of and then ordered the goods from Amazon and had them delivered via courier to where the homeless person was sitting. Mind blown...and I hope to replicate this level of ingenuity and irrational generosity in the future.

CORE WORK

We need to think about the core traits that we want to teach our children, like courage, loyalty, and faith that Andy Andrews writes about in *The Noticer Returns: Sometimes You Find Perspective, and Sometimes Perspective Finds You*. I try to show them courage to do the right thing even when the right thing is difficult to do. We were in Lowe's, the home improvement store, for example, and I got all the way back out to the car in the far corner of the parking lot with all four kids when I noticed a little bag of washers that the cashier missed. My kids wouldn't have known, but I brought it up.

"Guys, we've got to go back to the store," I said. "We

walked out and didn't pay for these washers. I think one of you was standing on top of them in the cart."

"I can't believe you came back in here and paid for those," the attendant even said after we walked all the way back in to pay for the washers. "No one would've known, and it wouldn't have been a big deal, but thank you for doing that."

That was a moment of doing the right thing. It really wasn't that difficult, but it was a chance to model that behavior for my kids. It was a teachable moment.

It's also important to build loyalty—loyalty to family, to country, to friends, to their school, and to their employer one day. I like to say that "the hardest promise to keep is the one that you don't want to." My daughter is a competitive hip-hop dancer, so she has classes a couple of nights a week with her team to build their routines. If she misses a class, she gets behind, and that can pull the whole team down because it's competitive in nature. It can even cause her to potentially to be taken off the team. This year she also wanted to play school volleyball, which we agreed to knowing there was going to be some overlap. Many times she had to make a choice. Who am I going to be loyal to, my school or my hip-hop team? She chose to go to hip-hop when she had those overlaps, recognizing she couldn't do both. The importance of being loyal to what she committed to first is one thing we've ingrained in our kids.

The final core trait we try to demonstrate for our children is faith, faith in God, faith in their family, faith in their friendships, faith in your church, and most importantly, faith in other people. As a society we have become so quick to take offense. We're so untrusting as a society. We're untrusting of our government. We're untrusting of our educational system. We're untrusting of our employers and other companies, and other people in general. I believe the antidote to that is faith. While it's important not to be naïve, it's important to have faith in all of those things. It starts with a positive viewpoint and open mind, and then extending that to the appropriate extent.

The intrinsic benefit of all of this modeling is that it creates accountability for you as a father. You're going to eat right, you're going to exercise, you're going to engage in the use of digital technology appropriately, and you're going to manage your finances the right way. You'll be more mindful of bad decisions or actions and correct them because it's important for your children to see you make mistakes, too, but then take ownership of them. They're watching you with those open eyes to see what you're doing ALL THE TIME, and if you're not aware of that, then you missed the opportunity. I'm sure you've heard the adage, "You are who you really are by the way you act when no one's looking." As a father, your kids are always looking and waiting to catch the behaviors you're demonstrating, positive or negative, so you don't have a moment where no one's looking. Your kids are always watching, soaking you up like a sponge. Are you the YOU your kids are looking for?

CHAPTER SIX

CREATING EPIC MOMENTS

*Epic   adjective | \ 'e-pik *

a: Extending beyond the usual or ordinary, especially in size and scope.

b: HEROIC

It was a fall morning in the Carolinas, and a thin layer of dew coated the grass on a football field behind our home. I had gone to Play It Again Sports the night before and bought a ski-boat inner tube. I woke the kids up early, dressed them in sweatshirts, and told them to grab their bike helmets. We walked outside to our golf cart where they saw the inner tube and began asking, "Dad, what in the world are we doing?" I left them full of suspense as we drove the golf cart over to a local football field. I hooked the inner tube rope to the back of the golf cart and asked, "Who's up first?" Mason jumped in the tube, strapped on his helmet, and Blane and Easton sat on the back of the golf cart with a GoPro. I put the pedal down and proceeded to pull Mason across the wet grass on the field, slinging him from side to side in the tube as if he was being pulled behind a ski boat on the water. His eyes were as big as saucers the first turn or two and then he settled in and was screaming like he was on an amusement park ride. I spent the balance of two hours pulling them across the field and they had the time of their lives. The tube cost me $20, but the epic memories we created that morning are priceless.

Now, I know what you're thinking: Maybe I can create an epic event once or twice a year but you're telling me, Justin, that I have to do that every Saturday? That sounds great in theory, but in practicality it's difficult to wrap my head and my hands around that. But you can do it if you just remember a couple of other 'E' words. Epic does not have to be expensive. It does not have to be extravagant. And epic does not necessarily have to be experiential. It just has to be engaging. Epic can simply be the fact that you're together with your children in an intentional setting, and that will be epic in their eyes. The biggest challenge is getting over any initial fear or insecurity to engage your kids. If you can do that, then these moments just naturally tend to become epic.

Why do certain memories stay with us while others seem to fade away? When you look back at your childhood, what memories stand out to you and have the stickiness factor allowing you to recall them years later? I can think back to certain defining moments in my life and almost all of them have my parents attached to them. When I think about what made these defining moments stand out to me, it's the fact they were elevated in my mind due to the epic nature of the memory. I also have a deep emotional connection with the memory and it elicits the same emotion years later. Don't miss this: the really interesting point is it's not the few single big memories that form the defining moments of how I view my childhood. It's the culmination of all the small and big memories added up to create the overall defining moment of how I view my childhood. The take home point here is don't forgo the small moments like epic Daddy Saturdays for a few big moments. The culmination of the little moments has more impact, long term, on how your kids will view their childhood.

We sometimes forget as adults that everything is bigger when you are a child. Remember as a child the first time you went to the ocean, walked through a forest, went to a sporting event, or visited Disney World? As we grow older our sense of curiosity and instant amazement seems to diminish as we become more desensitized to the world around us. This desensitization makes it more difficult to connect with our children and create epic moments because we tend to think through our adult eyes, rather than through the eyes of a child.

I want to be very clear in defining the word "epic," because as I look at my Daddy Saturdays, while we strive to create these epic moments, they're not all "mind-blowing." But just by the fact that we're together, having fun, smiling and laughing, we're stockpiling positive memories together. It just naturally becomes epic. It's all about the memories that you make together, and that's a really important point, because in today's society, I believe we've lost our identity in terms of our story and what's going to create the epic narrative for our own lives, for us, and for our children. It's vital we create epic memory burns.

My fear is the digital generation that's growing up, their epic moments are coming from in front of a screen, like we discussed in the previous chapter. In fact, if you search "epic moments" on Google, before you can even finish typing, Google populates it for you with "epic moments **fortnite**." *Fortnite* is an incredibly popular game that's taken over the world, but we have chosen not to let our kids play it at home. They may play it over at their friends' houses, and they all know the dances that the avatars can do—they've tried to teach me the Floss—but it's not something we engage in at home because I simply don't want the distraction. I know some fathers who say playing video games with their children is a valuable relationship-building tool because they are able to spend time with their kids doing something their kids enjoy. Call me old fashioned, but I find it hard to connect with my kids when I'm staring at a screen and not into their eyes.

As a society we are obsessed with other people's lives. From reality TV to YouTube videos to social media channels, you can access someone else's life so easily and forget to live your own. The bigger point here is that rather than consuming other people's stories, we should be creating our own as a parent with our children. We need to lift our eyes from the screen, remove our faces from behind the camera, and be fully present with our children. We need to engage our kids' curiosity and imagination to create their story and the narrative we want as a parent. As I've said before, the days are so long, but the years are so short. We have limited time with our kids in the home. What are we depositing in their memory banks that they're going to take with them when they leave the home in the way of great memories with their dad?

ANY GIVEN SATURDAY

Before I detail how you can create an epic experience, I want to simplify the concept for you. Playing catch with a baseball or football in the backyard is epic in your kids' eyes, especially if you compliment them and show a level of excitement when they make that catch, or you set up the scenario: "It's fourth and long, the game's on the line. Go deep," and then they catch it. "The crowd goes wild." The look in a kid's eyes is epic in and of itself. It's amazing when you engage your kids in that way, and they see that you're fully present, you're fully there, and you're making them the hero of the story in that moment. Something as small as playing catch in the backyard can be an epic memory between father and son or father and daughter.

If you have the opportunity, I highly recommend making your home into an epic playground of sorts. It doesn't take much, and you certainly don't need to do what we were blessed to do, but I just found it's better to stick as close to home as possible because when you leave the house, money flows. We bought and remodeled a 1950s ranch home that happened to have an old rundown, 1,000-square-foot barn in the back, which was a workshop we've turned into a pool house/guesthouse. We made an intentional decision as a family to forgo some additions to the home and instead invest in a swimming pool and outdoor living. With four children, our priority was to create incredible memories instead of having the most updated master bedroom and bath. We were blessed financially to be able to make these improvements to our home and try to be a good steward with what we've been given. Our home has become the neighborhood hangout and it's not uncommon to find ten or more kids playing in our backyard at any time. It brings Heather and me such joy to be able to have kids at our home playing and making memories. Daddy Saturday at home is the best way to save money and still create epic moments.

You may recall a commercial for an insurance company where the father is mowing the lawn on a hot summer day. The sun is beating down. His daughter is begging to go to a friend's house because she's bored out of her mind, and the dad just starts fantasizing about having a pool. As the family splashes and has fun in their new pool, a female voice says, "Tomorrow's important, but so is making the most of the house before they're out of the house." That sums up exactly how we feel. We made a choice to experience life now and to create those kinds of memories with our kids.

Our backyard looks like something out of the movie *Billy Madison* where he's got a pool and all these toys and games. (I don't have a red lobster float but may need to acquire one.) We're not quite to that extreme, but on any given Saturday, you're going to see our backyard turn into some crazy idea that we're engaging in that day. Often times, it just involves the permanent structures we have there—the pool and the Springfree Trampoline, which has just been an incredible asset for our family. The number of games that we've created on that trampoline and the time we've spent on it have just been invaluable, so many epic moments. It got to the point where my kids wouldn't jump on the trampoline unless I was with them, because it was more fun when Dad was on it, too. That in and of itself was such a great reward for me. I bought the kids headgear and boxing gloves, so it's become an Ultimate Fighting Championship octagon, where the boys can go in there and duke it out. In fact, one time we did "Daddy Saturday Boxing Edition." Hayden even took part. She's a southpaw, so I taught her how to throw a left hook, and she took all of her brothers down. It was lights out with her mean left hook. It was epic for a young girl to beat up her brothers in a controlled environment. She reminds them constantly that she can beat them up at any time.

We've also hung slack lines, which are these nylon lines that you ratchet between trees, so the kids can try to tight-rope walk across them and bounce on them. And I can't tell you the number of obstacle courses that we've built in our backyard. Typically, we're just using things that we find around the house. We have a kind of *American Ninja Warrior*/Spartan Race obstacle course with ropes, hanging rings, and other things that you can swing on. Tell your kids you're building an obstacle course in the yard and they will lose their minds! It's never failed me and is always epic to them, especially when they're young. It can be the smallest ramp or platform with a couple of

2x4s and a piece of wood tied together. When they have to go over it on their bike, it seems like it's the biggest ramp in the world to them. And because dad built it, it makes it even better. I am the least handy guy in the world, so if I can do it, anybody can do it.

I have to admit that coming up with a fresh, new, epic idea each and every Saturday doesn't come naturally to me. I dedicate time each week and particularly on Friday mornings to plan for the day ahead with my children. Early on, I was a little insecure about engaging my kids this way, but eventually I overcame the fear because the fear of failing as a father was a greater driving force. The is no shortage of access to ideas online for how parents can engage their kids, but there are many more ideas generated by and for mothers. Even some of the ideas for dads are generated by mothers. This is a big reason why I decided to write this book and take the Daddy Saturday platform public. If I can help dads engage their children and overcome the physical and mental barriers to doing so, then I feel like I've accomplished what I was put on this earth to do.

In order to make this easier on dads, I've developed the *Daddy Saturday Playbook* including fifty-two ideas—one for each Saturday of the year—on our bonus site listed at the end of the chapter. Let me give you examples of some of our favorite Daddy Saturday ideas that are included in the *Daddy Saturday Playbook*. One of my kids' favorite epic ideas only cost a few dollars and was absolutely hilarious. I bought almost every roll of jumbo bubble wrap they had at Lowe's and bubble wrapped the kids into what looked like large sumo suits. I also made jousting sticks out of bubble wrap, too, then I put them on the trampoline, and we had a bubble-wrap battle where they literally just ran and crashed into each other. The most humorous part was that they looked like they had giant bubble wrap diapers on instead of sumo suits. The suit on my second son, Mason, who was about four at the time, was so big that he looked like a turtle. He kept falling over and couldn't get back up! He would just lay on his back and call for help. The others were in hysterics. My kids will never forget the day that. It was so simple and so fun. All it took was a little bit of thought. The idea was so good we had to repeat it a year later, and we've also done a bubble-wrap obstacle course.

Another idea that the kids absolutely love is a taste test challenge or blind taste tests with all sorts of different types of condiments. It usually ends in a whipped cream fight. It costs hardly anything, and it's so much fun. We're also huge fans of Nerf. We have a collection of Nerf guns, and I found that you can order thousands of Nerf darts off Amazon for practically nothing. I've grown so accustomed to seeing Nerf darts in our home and our yard that they've become an accessory to our interior and exterior decorating. My only wish is that Nerf would invent technology that allowed the darts to return to sender so pickup would be easier! We've absolutely taken Nerf to the next level and used it in so many different epic trick-shot battles and Nerf wars.

These ideas may not come to you naturally, just as they don't come to me naturally. I spend time scrolling social media or browsing YouTube researching ideas. My goal is not to make them extravagant, just creative. Remember, you don't have to take your kids to Disney World, or an amusement park, or on vacation for it to be epic. Extravagance does not equal epic. Now, there have been times where it's been extremely extravagant. We've taken a big trip, and that's certainly been epic, but the backyard times have rivaled the epic nature of the most extravagant and expensive memories that we have. When in doubt, keep it simple and use the resources at your disposal. I've used glow sticks in more ways than you could ever imagine. The local party store is a great resource, so is The Dollar Store and Five Below, where nothing is over $5. Amazon, of course, is another great tool, and so is vat19. com, which has some crazy products like extreme gummy worms and invisible drums.

EPIC FAILS

Let me be real for a minute and show you something

outside the highlight reel. While I always hope Daddy Saturdays are epic, once in a while I have an epic fail. There have been many Saturdays where the only thing epic was my failure. There have been times where my ideas and my imagination were far beyond my capabilities. There were times where we had to call an audible and do something else, like the weather didn't permit us to do our original idea, but many times those turned out to be some of our best Daddy Saturdays. Even in times of failure, my kids have never been disappointed in me for trying. I've only been disappointed in myself for not pulling off the idea or preparing enough in advance.

While there have been many, let me share two of the most epic Daddy Saturday fails. One Saturday I had planned to do several activities on the trampoline, including a sprinkler/water balloon bounce off. I remember waking up and something was just off with the way my body was feeling. Heather had already left to work at her bridal store three hours away and I was home alone with the kids as usual until late in the evening. We got everything ready and proceeded to begin jumping on the trampoline. My body was extremely achy and I had zero energy, to the point I eventually just laid face down on the trampoline and let the kids bounce all around me. I was not my usual self and the kids kept asking, "What's wrong with you Daddy?" Finally, we ended up going inside and the kids watched movies all day while I was in bed. Turns out I had the flu and pneumonia! On another occasion I didn't do my prep work and tried to pull off a Daddy Saturday on the fly. I zoomed around the house on a Saturday morning and decided it would be fun to have a Play-Doh building contest. We used the Play-Doh we had in the house which was all mixed up in multi-colored hard chunks. After about five minutes the kids looked at me and said, "Dad, can we do something else for Daddy Saturday?" After I lit myself on fire I came back in and told the kids to throw the Play-Doh away and that we were going for ice cream! My kids are savvy and yours probably are too. They could tell I didn't have a plan and it wasn't one of my best efforts. The great thing about ice cream is it covers a multitude of failures.

Even when Daddy Saturdays do work, I need to point out that my kids aren't always like, "Dad, that was the most amazing experience ever." That's not the point. The point is that you're creating those memory burns and you're adding deposit after deposit with your kids while you have them, and you're forming them and structuring them. They're all not going to be epic, but if you add them all up, that's what's epic. The storybook you're creating with your children is epic.

I should also point out our Daddy Saturdays aren't usually more than a few hours together. To entertain your kids for the whole day, that's a big ask. Although we also happen to film it and create content around it that we post on YouTube and Instagram, that's not something you have to do. Your role is to just engage in the moment. That's what's important. But be forewarned: fathers engaging their kids in epic ways is so rare they're like unicorns, and other kids will want to be included. I can't tell you the number of neighborhood kids who want to be a part of Daddy Saturday and get on our YouTube channel. I've also been humbled and honored to inspire other parents both nationally and internationally who have now started to do Daddy Saturdays with their own kids. Kids are just craving this kind of intentional time with their own dads. There's a deep desire to have this level of engagement with their father. Our kids want time and attention from us, whether they admit it or not, and most times they're not going to. Remember that feelings follow behaviors, behaviors don't follow feelings, even with children. Trust me on this, if you engage your kids, it will become epic.

When kids engage with their parents, they feel valued and loved, which is vital in the developmental process. There are rewards for fathers, too. I have found that there are moments in these settings where I'll have the opportunity just to sit back and observe my children, observe their talents, their skills, their personalities, their nature, and the way they interact with each other. I have learned so much about my children and about the way I need to be as a parent toward them, just by being a part of these moments. There are things that I never, ever would have perceived otherwise.

Being present and engaged also enhances communication and the relationship bond. We've talked a lot about the accumulation of memories over time and in those moments, and the whole is greater than the sum of the parts. The key piece is there's this natural desire to have the father be involved in the life of a child, to have the father be there as a parent, as a coach, as a mentor, as a leader, and as a nurturer. That's what you get as a byproduct of these moments.

My favorite question to ask people is, "What's your story?" Is what you're doing with your children today going to allow them as adults to answer the above question with clarity and certainty? As fathers we need to create a generation of creators and curators, not consumers. As fathers let's step up, be intentional, be engaged, and use our God-given talents to help our children write their own epic story. Someone or something in our culture is going to step up and fill that void. If not you, then who?

BONUS MATERIAL

Want a free e-book filled with fifty-two epic ideas for how to engage your children each week? Go to our bonus site to download the free *Daddy Saturday Playbook*. The *Daddy Saturday Playbook* even includes links to Amazon for each activity so you can source the necessary supplies without even leaving the house! Go to www.DaddySaturday.com/bonus

CHAPTER SEVEN

WINNERS TRAVEL

"Each day of our lives we make deposits in the memory banks of our children."

—CHARLES R. SWINDOLL, AUTHOR AND
FOUNDER OF INSIGHT FOR LIVING

As a 2002 graduate of Clemson University, I'm a huge fan of all things Clemson Tigers (2016 & 2018 College Football National Champions), and I was talking to another fan and mentor, Dr. Clay Lowder, who told me this story about when Evander Holyfield, the famous boxer, came in and spoke to the football team a few years back. Holyfield's message was that "winners travel" because that's what Clemson was doing by traveling to the ACC Championship, as well as to the College Football Playoffs. Evander was espousing the principle that winners don't stay home; winners are on the road making it happen in sports, business, and life. After Clay finished telling me the story about Evander speaking to Clemson, he began telling me how he had adopted a similar concept in his life and with his family over the years. Clay made it an intentional habit to take family vacations because, in the words of Evander, "winners travel." When Clay shared this with me, I had a hard time staying in my seat. The concept lit me on fire, and I knew it was something I had to do immediately with my family.

The concept of Winners Travel didn't fully take shape in my mind until the summer of 2018 when I met a gentleman by the name of Dean Akers, a successful CEO who also did a wonderful job helping to raise five good children who are all now great adults. We started talking about the challenges and joys of raising good kids who become great adults when I told him about my Daddy Saturday platform. Dean looked at me and said:

"Are you ready to take it to the next level?"

I was little shocked at first because I felt like I had already done that but politely said, "Of course. What do you have in mind?"

He then went on to explain how he took each of his children on "Just Us Trips" at age ten, thirteen, and sixteen. At ten, they could choose a destination anywhere in the U.S. just for the two of them, and at thirteen and sixteen, it was anywhere in the world. The kids could also do anything they wanted while on the trip and Dad couldn't say "no." What really stuck with me, however, was his comment that whenever he gets together with his grown children, the stories of their "Just Us Trips" come up every single time. It's one of the things they remember the most from their childhoods. I still get chill bumps just writing about that moment, as it was yet another time where a person was placed in my life and contributed significantly to my purpose. Like most of you reading this, my mind instantly went to, *Can I afford to do this?* I'm not a successful CEO, and I'm not sure if I can swing three trips, including two international trips, with my four kids! However, where there's a will there's a way, as the saying goes, and I knew deep down this was something I couldn't afford NOT to do. The memory burns and defining moments would be priceless, and I thought, *This is exactly what I was looking for as a way to take my relationship with my kids to the next level.*

While the meeting with Dean occurred in late summer of 2018, it just so happened that my daughter, Hayden Olivia, turned eleven on November 21, 2018, so I had limited time to plan her ten-year-old trip. Needless to say, when I introduced the concept of Winners Travel to my kids, they lost their minds and it got them so excited. They've all started thinking about and researching places they want to go, even four-year-old Easton. It didn't take

Hayden long to choose the Big Apple, New York City, for her first trip. She had never been to New York and had heard so much about it from Heather and me from our trips there. She also loves arts and culture, so top on her list was to see her first Broadway show. With no time to spare, we immediately got to work planning the trip. The first thing I did was crowdsource my LinkedIn network to ask contacts who live and work in New York for their advice and inside tips because I really wanted to make this trip something she'd always remember. I know just the memories and the time we would have one-on-one would be epic, but I wanted Hayden to have the best experience possible so she would walk away feeling really special. My network really came through, like suggesting we stay at Hotel Hayden (her namesake...really?), which is located on West 28th Street between 6th and 7th Avenues in the city's stylish Chelsea district. They provided recommendations on shows, where to eat, and what to see while we were in town. I'm very grateful for the advice and the power of putting a social network like LinkedIn to good use.

APPLE OF MY EYE

Before we knew it, the trip was upon us. Heather and the boys dropped us off at the airport, and you could see the pride in Heather's eyes. The boys were certainly a bit jealous, but they knew their turn would come and had already begun throwing out destinations for their ten-year trip. We took off from Charleston and flew into LaGuardia on a Thursday night. She was glued to the window as we approached the city, looking at all of the lights of Manhattan below with her eyes wide open, a look that rarely left her face. She had one great surprise after another, starting with seeing her name on the hotel as we pulled up in our Uber. Of course, when we checked in I introduced her to the front desk clerk.

"Hi, this is Hayden, and she will be staying here at The Hotel Hayden."

The receptionist made a big fuss before I took some pictures of her in front of the Hotel Hayden sign. When we got to our room, there was a gift bag of Hotel Hayden swag waiting for her, like stationary, glasses, a water bottle, and a bunch of other goodies that were all emblazoned with her name. To see other people invested in her having an incredible trip just meant the world to me. Although it was late, we decided to take a stroll around Times Square so she could see all the lights. We concluded the day with dinner at the hotel and retired for the night with Hayden full of excitement for the coming surprises over the next few days.

After a workout together in the hotel gym, we went out to explore the city. She was completely enthralled with the pace and energy of the city as walked through midtown Manhattan. We visited Rockefeller Center and saw the ice rink with all the skaters and the famous Christmas tree. NBC studios is right there as well, so we got to see where one of our favorite entertainers, Jimmy Fallon, records *The Tonight Show*. She also did a little shopping— how can you not in New York City?—trying on fur coats, gold-emblazoned Michael Kors shoes, hats, glasses, and handbags, and was kind to her father by not asking to purchase a single one! That Friday night for dinner we went to Ellen's Stardust Diner, which is an incredible scene. All of the waiters and waitresses are Broadway hopefuls, and every couple of minutes, one of them just breaks into a Broadway show tune. They're bringing you your food one minute and singing a song the next. It's a fun atmosphere with confetti everywhere. Hayden loved it. It was the perfect place to go before she got to see her first Broadway show, *School of Rock*. We also saw *Wicked* (her top request), as well as *Dear Evan Hansen*. Three Broadway shows in three nights was quite an experience and made a lasting impression on her.

As I mentioned previously, Hayden is a competitive hip-hop dancer, so we did something called the Hush Hip Hop Tour, which was a tour of the history and the origins of hip hop that took us from Manhattan to Harlem and then the Bronx, where it all began and where the National Museum of Hip Hop is located. Hayden was overjoyed when the professional dancer who led the tour showed us how to break dance in the lobby. We also did something called a dance cypher where everyone on the tour formed a circle, and we all had to take turns dancing in the middle. Hayden and I were about the last two to go. Of course, Hayden got in there and nailed it with all these great moves. Then it was my turn, and all I wanted to do was try and embarrass Hayden because it's one of my favorite things to do in those moments. I walked into the circle with a little swagger and then proceeded to do my best moves standing up before I leapt to the ground, spun on my back, and struck a break-dancer pose. The entire group went crazy, and Hayden was absolutely mortified during the process, so I achieved my goal. There may or may not be a video of that moment, but the tour was really special for Hayden. She got to see something that she loves, while also learning about its roots and what it means to generations past, as well as her generation.

GRATITUDE GAINED

Hayden was also exposed to many different cultures on the trip. Different types of people, cultures, languages, and food that she's never experienced before. There were so many things about the trip that were unexpected, which was the byproduct of being in New York. Another byproduct I didn't expect was the gratitude Hayden gained for living in Charleston, S.C. Now when I say, "Do you know how fortunate you are to live five minutes from the beach or have a swimming pool in your backyard?" it resonates a lot more. It's really difficult when you're trying to use that as leverage and they don't have any additional perspective. Now when I say that, it has true meaning because she's actually seen what the other side of that looks like.

On the last day, Sunday, we attended a church service at Hillsong NYC, a church that began in Australia and now has twenty-one churches worldwide with almost 130,000 weekly attendees. What an amazing experience that was. To be in downtown Manhattan and see that the line to get into the service was longer than the lines for Broadway was incredible, and the music and the energy at the church was equally as impressive as anything that we saw on Broadway. We told the Hillsong staff why we were in town, and they were so courteous to give us incredible seats just ten rows from the stage. Pastor Carl Lentz gave an inspiring message titled, "I will fight!" and I purchased a copy of his book, *Own the Moment*, afterwards (one of my favorite books of 2018). At the end of the service, Hayden and I walked down front and a staff member prayed over Hayden and encouraged her in her life. As a dad standing there watching someone pray over your daughter and speak life into her...I still have no words.

Our next stop was The Morgan Library & Museum,

where I had set up a private tour. This is the museum of Pierpont Morgan, who was the founder and namesake of JP Morgan, of course, and an avid art collector. His home is also part of the tour, as well as an annex and a few other buildings that house both his library and art collection. In addition to seeing some priceless art and rare cultural artifacts, we also saw some of the original Bibles, as well as rare, single-edition books. We stood in his office, which is lined with red velvet wallpaper and has this massive fireplace in it. We learned the story of how during the Great Depression he called in all the top financiers and bankers in the United States into that room, which they weren't allowed to leave until they figured out a plan for how to get America out of the Great Depression. I'm not sure if Hayden appreciated the moment as much as I did, but at the same time she got this amazing indoctrination into art history and culture. That night, before going to see *Wicked*, we had dinner in Little Italy. The restaurant knew she was coming, and they treated her like a princess. Every step along the way, I looked for little ways to take it up a notch or make it more special. But perhaps the highlight for Hayden was seeing *Wicked*, where we sat front and center, five rows back.

The highlight for me as a father was getting to spend so much one-on-one time with my daughter. It was invaluable. I learned so much about her that I miss on a daily basis because we're moving so fast and my attention is also spread out amongst her brothers. It's a different dynamic when you are one-on-one and the level of connection is so much deeper. One thing I learned, for instance, is that she doesn't like to be rushed. She was a bit exhausted after our whirlwind weekend, and I was having trouble motivating her to get ready to get to the airport.

"Hayden, we have to leave for the airport," I remember telling her. "We're going to be late for our flight. We've got to go!"

And she just started to shut down and forget things. I had seen that behavior before, but it was typically in the context of getting ready for school, and that's when a light went off for me.

"You don't like to be rushed, do you?" I asked her. "You shut down."

"No, I don't like to be rushed at all," she responded. "It makes me feel really uncomfortable, and I start to forget things when you and Mom push me like that."

I then asked her what she thought we could do differently, and she said that she could have packed the night before, so we have translated that to our home life now. But I only saw the behavior because of the one-on-one situation. I was able to zoom out, see it in a different context, and now I can approach the issue completely differently. It was a game changer for our relationship because there are many times when we have trouble motivating her to get moving. I can't believe it took me taking a trip to New York to figure that out, but it did.

The second thing that came out of this trip was just the communication we have, the level of communication now between us is so much better. Our bond is much stronger, where I can give her a glancing look and she knows what I'm thinking. Hayden's a "preenager" and communicating with her has become more of a challenge than it's been with my boys. She has a quiet nature. She's introspective and introverted. She isn't outwardly expressive like I am or like some of my other kids, so often in our daily routines, I'll get the impression that she's not having fun or she's not engaged or she's not enjoying the experience, but she completely is. She just processes it differently.

And so, while we have incredible memory burns experiencing one of the biggest cities in the world together, three Broadway shows in three nights, and everything else, it was those little things in the margins that meant the most to me and will be the building blocks for our relationship going forward.

TIME IS OF THE ESSENCE

Now, I realize everybody doesn't have the means to do this kind of trip and Winners Travel doesn't have to be extravagant. The point is just to take your kids outside of your normal environment and spend one-on-one time with them. The reason I went into so much detail for you regarding our New York trip is because I hoped to convey the level of intentionality that went into the trip. The time and cost are irrelevant. You could go camping for a few days. The point is that you just get out of your natural element and create an environment where you have this space in the margin to zoom out and experience that time together, as well as creating defining moments that turn into lasting memory burns. Hayden will remember so much about this trip that has nothing to do with the fact that we went to New York. It's the fact that we planned the whole thing together, I took time out of my schedule, and we spent quality time together. I invested in her and our relationship, and the win here is it's more about the investment of time. That's what really matters with Winners Travel. It's also inspired me to think that I don't need to wait for ten, thirteen, and sixteen to engage in that one-on-one time. It's encouraged me to think, *How do I take time every week, even if it's just for fifteen or thirty minutes?*

The boys are already starting to think about where they want to go when they turn ten. That's been great fun in the house just to even be able to talk about that and for them to have something to look forward to. Blane has already told me he wants to go to Dallas to visit the headquarters of Dude Perfect, a hugely popular group of trick-shot guys who post all their stunts on YouTube and have become internet superstars. A lot of our Saturdays have been themed or based off ideas that they have created, so they've been a great indirect contributor to Daddy Saturday.

When I look back on my role as a father and my kids have all grown and gone, I don't want to have any regrets. I am so grateful to Dean Acres and Clay Lowder because they eliminated one of the potential regrets I wasn't even aware of had they not planted the Winners Travel seed. I'm now on pace to do this with all of my children. That's twelve trips in all, but when I look at my body of work as a father, my dad's résumé, if you will, these are going to be some of those bigger bullet points that I can look back at and say, "Those are significant investments, significant moments in the lives of my children." I'm sure there will be stories that we will tell again and again over the years, just as Dean's grown children do today, and hopefully it becomes a tradition where my kids do the same thing with their kids.

Now, you're probably wondering how Heather feels about being left out of all this fun, but she sees exactly how it fits into the concept of Daddy Saturday and building good kids who become great adults. We are so aligned in our mission and the vision for what we want for our children, and what we want for each other as parents that, anytime something like this comes up, it's not about me versus you or you get to do this and I don't. It's about how does it apply to where we want our kids ultimately to be. That's the bigger picture. It also helps that we take at least four "just us" trips each year as well to invest in our marriage. Of course, Hayden Olivia is her only daughter and she's joked about how jealous she is, especially when I'm texting her photos of Hayden shopping in the best and biggest stores in Manhattan, but at the same time she and Hayden have had plenty of one-on-one time together. I'm all for moms doing the same thing and creating one-on-one time or trips with their kids. However, there's just something special about a dad traveling one-on-one with his kids, and if as a father you are willing to take the risk, there's a great reward waiting for you.

It's also important to note it's never too late to take trips with your children, even if they're in their late teens or twenties; the experience will bring you closer. This is my calling and my challenge for all fathers to think differently and step it up. There's a very specific and unique role that fathers play in the lives of their kids who absolutely crave time with their dads, and there's no better way to give them that than on a trip where you can completely engage with your child individually and disengage from everything and everyone else.

If you bring the principle of Winners Travel into your parenting, it will create milestone defining moments your children will speak about for the rest of their lives. When you add Winners Travel defining moments into the daily intentional moments and the weekly epic Daddy Saturdays, you have three critical ingredients for the recipe of how to raise good kids who become great adults.

BONUS MATERIAL

Want a guide for how to pull off an epic trip with your children? Go to our bonus site to download the free Daddy Saturday *Winners Travel Guide*. Go to www.DaddySaturday.com/bonus

CHAPTER EIGHT

A DAD'S COMPASS

"Direction, not intention, determines destination."

—ANDY STANLEY, AUTHOR AND FOUNDER
OF NORTH POINT MINISTRIES

My family and I were recently in Jacksonville, Florida, for a Spartan Race and the area we were racing in was very remote. After the race we had about a twenty-minute drive to get back to the interstate for our trip home. We were leaving the parking lot and my cell phone, Heather's cell phone, and my father's cell phone all had no service. You would have thought the world ended as the three of us continued to try to refresh Google Maps to get our directions back to the interstate. We were literally paralyzed without directions and didn't know whether to go left or right. The way we got moving again was by using the compass in the iPhone to head in the direction we needed to go. I also made a vow to pick up a good ole

Rand McNally Atlas just in case that ever happens to us again.

How often in life and parenting do you also feel like you are paralyzed by a lack of direction? As a father there will be many forks in the road where you must determine whether to go left or right and the outcome of your choice can carry large consequences. Perhaps as a father you feel like you are making it up as you go. It's ok to feel that way, and I believe most of us enter our role as a parent that way. Many of us parent by default. You may have the best of intentions to be a great dad, but there's so much in your life that can take you off course. There are many factors pulling you away from the initial ideals you've set for your marriage, family, and role as a father. For example, you may have set the intention to respond in a kind and caring way to your children, but then the stress of a long day gets the better of you and instead you explode at them. In the heat of the moment, intentions are irrelevant because the direction you're pointed in takes over. If you ultimately want your kids to become great adults, you have to do a lot more than state your intentions. You must have a compelling and bold vision for where you want your kids to go. You have to have a true north, a *Dad Compass* of sorts that points you in the right direction.

One way you can begin forming a *Dad Compass* is by laying out a specific mission statement for your family.

Our entire family sat down and we developed a family mission statement. Heather and I also have a mission statement for our marriage and individually as a mother and father regarding how we want to raise our kids. We also developed a "painted picture" of specifically what our family will look like twenty years from now. I start the painted picture by describing the fact I'm reading the letter at our annual Batt Family Memory Burn on a specific tropical island. I then begin to detail everything that's occurred leading up to that point in time to the current state to include where we live, the marital status of our children, the number of grandkids, the vacations we've taken, and so on. You get the idea—it just needs to be specific toward exactly what you desire your family to look like in the future. (See the bonus section at the end of the chapter for resources on how to create a family and fatherhood mission statement and painted picture). As you think about your mission statement and painted picture, envision your children in their twenties doing something they're passionate about, employing their strengths and their talents. They've got a great spouse and are great parents themselves. They're strong in their faith, they're strong in their family, and they're strong in their career. They're physically healthy and active—all the things you've tried to build over the years. You may find it helpful to actually write stories for all of your children describing them in their twenties and thirties and what you want and imagine for them. If you see it, you can achieve it and you've got to be really explicit with your vision.

To help truly identify a vision for your children, it's vital you ask the right questions. I'll give you a great example. Hayden is very musically inclined. She loves dance, she loves theater, and is so passionate about the arts, but to know if that's the right path for her, leadership coach and author Marshall Goldsmith recommends asking active questions, not passive ones. Instead of asking, "Hayden, do you enjoy dance?" I asked her, "Hayden, tell me how you feel when you're on the dance floor." And she said, "I feel like my whole body just comes alive. I feel free. If I had a bad day, it all just goes away when I'm dancing." A response like that lets you know you've really hit their passion point. That's something you can really grab onto and encourage as a parent. This even works with younger kids like my son Easton who is four. Instead of asking, "Easton, how was your day?" to which he will always say, "Good!" I ask him, "Easton, what was the best part of your day today?" or, "If you could do one thing differently today what would it be?" I am continually amazed by his responses even at four years old.

Another great leader and motivational author whom I've had the pleasure of meeting is Pat Williams, one of the founders of the Orlando Magic and former coach who led his teams to twenty-three NBA Playoffs and five NBA

Finals. He's also an incredible father who has raised nineteen children, fourteen of whom were adopted, so Pat knows a thing or two about parenting and fatherhood. He loves to play a game with his kids called "would you rather?"

"Would you rather go to a college in the North or the South, in warm or cold weather? Would you rather go to dinner at a really nice restaurant on your first date or just go get pizza?"

I've employed this in my family because it's a great way to make use of dead time if you're waiting somewhere or you're in the car, and the kids really enjoy sharing their answers. But it also helps you—and them—identify what they gravitate toward and frame that picture in their minds. The deeper you go, the clearer the picture and the plan it takes to execute it.

"Alright, you've told me that by the time you're twenty-three, you want to graduate from Clemson University with a business degree at the top of your class and you want to work on Wall Street. Okay, so how do we get there? What is it going to take for you to do that?"

The vision my wife and I have for them is the same vision every parent probably has for their children: to be healthy, happy, successful, and to find your God-given purpose in life. It's entirely possible to be successful but miss the purpose for your life. My job as their father is not to choose their occupation for them or tell them who their spouse should be. My job is to help them build a bold, purpose-filled mission for their life and if they find it, the rest will take care of itself.

What Pat Williams gave me is pure gold because you can do it with a four-year-old, a fourteen-year-old, or a twenty-four-year-old. Of course, the depth of the questions gets deeper the older they are, but it's all about alignment. It's such an easy way to help them, and guess what my kids do? They turn it around on me. They ask me the same questions, and it's so much fun because I get to tell my kids about my preferences, so they learn about me as well. Although this somehow never translates to their answers on the "about my dad" school projects...broccoli is not my favorite food, Easton! You can use the "would you rather?" game as a communication building tool. We've done this over the years and it continues to evolve and grow. The more you play the game, the more you get in touch with your kids' feelings because their preferences change. They start thinking about their answers at a deeper level, which allows you to peel back the layer of the onion a little bit and get to know them even better.

"Well, that's interesting, because last time you said you wanted to go to a southern school. Now you've changed your mind and you want to go to an Ivy League school, so what's changed? What made you come to that conclusion?"

You get to learn their thought process, their line of thinking that led them to their answer. It's really funny when you get into the husband or wife version of "would you rather," and who they see themselves marrying. Hayden, of course, says, "I want someone like you, Daddy," (Go ahead say, "Ahhhh") which I'm humbled by. My boys start blushing and there are a lot of "oh yeahs" and "ha ha's." The older boys, Blane and Mason, have said they want a blonde wife, which caused their brown-haired mom to say, "Hey, what's wrong with brunettes?" And they start laughing. Then, of course, Easton, the youngest, is like, "I want a brunette like you, Mommy." The "would you rather" game is such a simple tool to help identify the direction your kids want to set for themselves and it allows you to hold them accountable for their own vision and future.

CREATING ACCOUNTABILITY

The vision they create for themselves also helps hold them accountable. Hayden has said she wants to be the lead dancer in a top dance production on Broadway when she's twenty-five, so when she's not going to dance practice or she's not practicing outside of class, it's really easy to say, "Your dream is to be the lead dancer on a

Broadway show by age twenty-five. Do you think that only doing the number of hours that you're in class and not taking that home and practicing outside of class is going to get you to where you want to be?" I remind her this is her dream, not mine, so the accountability is on her. I'm not forcing her to do anything; it's up to her whether she wants to achieve her goal or not.

Same for my boys. Like most boys, they want to be professional athletes at this age, or they want to play sports at a collegiate level, so it allows me to remind them of their vision.

"You've got a choice: you can sit down and watch TV or play video games, and that's fine; you're a kid. I want you to be a kid, but ultimately you told me that this is your dream or your goal. Is what you're doing right now going to help you get to where you want to be?"

It's not about them going outside and practicing football drills at eight years old after school. It's just about getting them to think critically about their decisions and asking, "Is this going to get me where I want to go?" Instead of me saying, "Hey, shut the TV off and go outside," it's a simpler conversation. It's up to them whether they want to turn the TV off, go outside, and make the choice for themselves.

There is so much noise surrounding our children on a

constant basis, it's really easy for them to be distracted and do a whole lot of nothing for a whole lot of their childhood, which isn't going to lead them to where they want to go in life. The biggest concern I have for my children and all future children is they are living in a state of distractedness for the most formative years of their life. I'm not saying kids should be involved in every activity in the world and never be a kid and have no downtime where you manufacture a professional athlete or dancer or scientist or mathematician. But if you don't have a vision for your kids, and your kids don't have a vision for themselves, then you're missing out on a golden opportunity for them to become who they were meant to be, all because you weren't intentional about helping them paint their picture.

When you put these principles in place, you're also teaching your children the highly valuable trait of delayed gratification, and that's a really hard thing to do because we live in an immediate gratification society. I'm trying to take every chance I can get to find ways to help my kids delay gratification. If I can help them even slightly master delayed gratification, it will put them in the top 1 percent of society because no one else does this. In an Amazon Prime, next-day delivery society where we have access to anything, where we can watch a movie on demand, if I can teach my kids delayed gratification for what ultimately will benefit them in the long run, then they possess a skill set that will benefit them for the rest of their lives and give them an outsized advantage over anyone else, regardless of what they choose to do.

There was a study published in 1972 called "The Marshmallow Experiment" where a Stanford University psychologist by the name of Walter Mischel put hundreds of four- and five-year-olds separately in a room with a marshmallow on the table in front of them. A researcher offered each child a deal: don't eat the marshmallow during the fifteen minutes he was away and he would reward the child with a second marshmallow. The choice was clear: one treat right now or two treats later. The hilarious reactions ran the gamut from some kids jumping up and eating the marshmallow as soon as the researcher left to others doing the best to restrain themselves but eventually giving in. A few of the children did manage to wait the entire time, but the most interesting part came years later after the researchers tracked each child's progress in a number of areas over the course of four decades. Over and over again during that span, the group who waited patiently for the second marshmallow succeeded in whatever capacity they measured—SAT scores, substance abuse, obesity rates, and a range of other life measures. The takeaway is that success usually comes down to choosing the pain of discipline over the pleasure of immediacy, the very definition of what delayed gratification is all about.

CLIMBING THE STAIRCASE

As you walk along the journey following your *Dad Compass*, it's also important to constantly review your goals to keep them on pace. It goes back to that stair-step approach where my children's vision and my vision for them is sitting at the top of a giant staircase, and in order to get there we've got to take it one step at a time, one day at a time. Typically, when I sit down for breakfast with my kids, in order to win the day, I will ask them, "Hey, what's your goal for the day?" Often times, it's, "To get a good report in class," or in the case of Hayden, who plays volleyball and was struggling with her serve, it was, "Get every serve over the net tonight at my volleyball game." You may want to try this because it's a great way to begin embedding a goal-setting principle in your child's mind. I also try to model out goal setting for my kids in a number of ways, like training for Spartan Races. My kids know I just don't wake up on the day of the race and go do it. They've seen me get up at the crack of dawn for months to train for the race. I also include them in my training on the weekends, so when they see me do the race and succeed, they saw all the effort that I put in to get to that point. It helps them understand with any goal, you have to break it down into bite-size pieces. I try to teach them you've got to win the day, and if you win the day, then you win the week, and if you win the week, then you win the month, and if you win the month, then you win the year. When you start stacking those years on top of each other, that's how you climb the staircase.

In the end, dads need to treat their family life like they do their business life. Just about any successful business today has a mission statement, core values, key objectives, and goals. Most successful companies have these plastered all around the walls of their company. We've done the same thing in our home with framed quotes and artwork from people like Dave Ramsey ("Live like no one else now, so you can live like no one else later") and Chip Gaines ("Live every day like it's Saturday"). These are signs and reminders of some of the core values and vision for our family. We need to apply the same effort and principles that we know leads to success in the office, in the home.

As a father who's married, I would be remiss if I didn't share the incredible benefit of doing a goal-setting vacation with your wife each year. Heather and I do this by getting away at the end of every year without the kids to spend two days goal setting for the next year, for the family as a whole and for us as individuals, all of which tie into our broader vision and long-term mission. We stay at a nice hotel, go on breakfast, lunch, and dinner dates, workout together, and spend hours communicating and working on our marriage. This year we went to Toronto, Canada, driving six hours each way from my parents' home in Ohio. We've found that car time is dangerous for us (in a good way) because we will create three new businesses and ten new things each we want to attain in the year ahead! We also combined this trip as not only a goal-setting trip, but to pick up our new family pet and Daddy Saturday mascot, "Weekend," a Bernedoodle from Swiss Ridge Kennels. We set our goals first, then we involve the kids so they have some input. One goal this year, for example, is to take two family vacations, so they got to weigh in on where we are going to go as a family, and then we write them down and create a budget. It's another great exercise to help your kids set their own goals.

We'll also often asked them as part of their goal setting, "What's one new skill you want to learn this year?" Blane wanted to learn how to surf last year, so we had to ask him, "How do you plan on getting there?" Well, first, he had to get a surfboard, but since his birthday is in November, he was going to have to buy one to catch the summer surf season, so we struck a deal where he would pay half of it, which he did by working and saving. There were so many principles that he learned just in the process of setting that one goal.

I don't leave much to chance because I only have one chance to be an intentional dad. I only have one chance to be successful at parenting. It's the most important thing in my life, and I want to encourage other dads to make it the most important thing in their lives, too. Sometimes all takes is a little bit of perspective and insight to be able to put it in place.

That's not to say I don't have regrets from my own life and opportunities missed—I do—so I learn from them, as I do from my own upbringing. I'm so thankful my parents gave me so many different experiences, but I look back and wish I had learned to play the guitar, for instance, or speak a foreign language. I don't force anything on my kids, but I do force the thought process to say, "Hey, later in life if you want to be in a band, or you want to play a musical instrument, you don't start that when you're eighteen because it's a lot harder. I bought a guitar when I was in my twenties, but I was a husband and father with a full-time job, so that guitar sits in my attic. I never learned how to play it because there were so many other demands of life that I couldn't commit the time necessary to do it. I'd rather have my kids say, "Yeah, Dad was probably a little bit over the top and pushed me, but at the end of the day, I am so thankful because I am where I want to be. I'm happy, healthy, and fulfilled because of all the vision and habits he helped me create early on in my life."

The road of raising children is filled with peaks and valleys, twists and turns, and there is no straight line to raising good kids who become great adults. Having a *Dad Compass* is the critical element to pointing your kids in the right direction, and then walking alongside them as their guide to help them keep moving toward their vision. If they deviate, you're there to gently redirect them back onto the narrow way by serving as their guide to their true north. There may be times where you have to get behind them and give them a little push, too, but before you know it, their own compass will take over and you can put yours away.

BONUS MATERIAL

Want free resources on how to create a family and fatherhood mission statement and how to write your own painted picture? Go to www.DaddySaturday.com/bonus

CHAPTER NINE

RAISING GOOD KIDS WHO BECOME GREAT ADULTS

"I'm not raising my kids to survive the world. I'm raising them to change it."

—STEVEN FURTICK, AUTHOR AND
FOUNDER OF ELEVATION CHURCH

"Do you like my stretchy pants?" I ask Heather as I walk by preparing to go for a run. "Please put on some shorts!" she hollers back at me as I make my way through the door without heeding her advice. I have on full length compression tights with no shorts over top and I don't care who sees me or what they think. I've even begun to wear them when I travel, although I do put shorts over top for that occasion. Women are on to something as they now wear yoga pants everywhere they go, why can't a guy wear stretchy pants too? My boys also all wear athletic tights under their shorts and I will never forget the look on Heather's face when they all rolled into the kitchen wearing their "stretchy pants" with no shorts over top. She looked at me like, now see what you've done! I just smiled and told the boys "nice tights." This is nothing new for me as I've always been the type of person who pushes the limits and grates against the norm. As I'm running the race of life, I'm constantly looking for new paths to take that will make the adventure even more fun.

The race of fatherhood is not won by the swift or the strong, but by the one who endures until the end. Now that you have a true-north vision for fatherhood, the final piece to the puzzle, when you're presented with a choice, is to ask yourself, *Does that align with my vision of myself as a father and where I want my kids to be?* If it doesn't, then you need to go in the other direction. When the world goes left, I go right, but it can be difficult to go against the grain. It seems everything has become so commoditized including parenting; how do you separate yourself from the pack? As I look at my kid's future and where I want them to go, I try to avoid the herd mentality because it's almost always the completely wrong way to go. If I want my kids to separate themselves and have a path for success in life where they become not just good kids but ultimately great adults, then it's never deviating from that true north heading, which often is the opposite direction of the way the world is going. I believe my children have the ability to change the generation they are alive in, and I believe your children have the potential to do the same. If you desire to align yourself with other fathers who share the same beliefs and have a similar velocity in the way they approach fatherhood, then I encourage you to join the countless other fathers in the Daddy Saturday movement.

HACKING THE SYSTEM

In order to raise good kids who become great adults, there are times you will have to go against the grain and even hack the system. Let me give you an example: Like a lot of people, we paid more money to buy a house in a neighborhood with good public schools, but then had second thoughts about sending our kids there because of the class size of more than twenty-five students. Two of my kids have moderate dyslexia, so they needed special services which weren't available in the public-school setting to the extent they needed them, so we made the decision to move our kids into a private Christian school where there are only about ten students per class. On paper, it made zero sense. We're paying more for our four kids to go to elementary school than we do for our home mortgage, but the public school wasn't aligned with what we wanted for our kids. Now our kids have more than enough resources, not only for the two who have dyslexia, but for all of my kids who are now hacking the standardized school system which does little to help children identify their areas of strength. Most importantly, because our children attend a Christian school, their faith is being enriched for six-plus hours a day instead of only at home or on Sundays. Heather, who used to be a teacher, has been instrumental in helping them formulate a better, more tailored curriculum, which we couldn't do in the public-school system.

My kids are gaining so much from being in that environment, and while it doesn't make sense financially now, I know that long term it's the right thing to do. It's going to get them ultimately where they want to be. While most people would justify sending their children the public-school route, we've chosen to go in a different direction and essentially hack the school system. We made a decision we feel is best for our family and certainly understand everyone has their own set of circumstances. The point here is to look at where your kids are spending six-plus hours a day and if there are gaps between what's being provided and what you envision for your child, then you need to address those. Technology does offer some benefits like online curriculums and there are many positive educational games to supplement your child's learning. However, I would caution you against adding any additional screen time unless it's the only option for learning. There are many different educational subscription boxes your child can receive monthly and are filled with computer programming, science experiments, arts and crafts, etc. If you use a little creativity, there are a multitude of resources available to help set your children on the path to achieve their dreams.

Our vision for our children has caused us to go against the norm in other ways, too. As I mentioned earlier about the overuse of technology, we cut the cable cord a long time ago and restrict the hours that our kids are in front of screens every day because of the harm overuse can cause. Our eating habits are also out of the norm. When you look at childhood obesity and see what families put in their shopping cart, it's mostly sugary, processed food. We're being lied to by the mass-marketed companies who put out products that are supposedly healthy for children, and they're actually terrible for them. We've educated our kids to say "no thank you" to foods that have artificial colors in them. They get some looks from other kids and their parents, but they've learned the harm they can cause. Perhaps you can look at your life and take an inventory of where you need to break from the norm in order to attain the long-term outcome you desire for your children.

NO FINGER POINTING (UNLESS IT'S AT THEMSELVES)

"Take that finger and turn it around!" is a common saying

in our household. I use this phrase to show my kids how not to have a victim mentality, which is a huge problem in our society today. A victim mentality can be defined as the belief that a person is not accountable for their own actions, that the government or the environment or the economy or their employer or their family upbringing or their father, you name it, is the reason why they're not where they want to be in life. It's a pervasive trend we see in our society today, and I am working very diligently to instill the opposite of the victim mentality, which is personal responsibility, in my children. There are many times in our household where something will happen and I'll find my children either making an excuse or placing blame on the environment or something or someone else. That's when I tell them to take their finger, turn it around, and point it back at themselves. *What can you do, or what could you have done to change that situation or to do things differently?* Many times, I will take their finger and turn it around for them if they don't do it themselves. It's a physical representation of accountability.

My three boys sleep in one room together in bunk beds. It's chaos, but they love it. It's the three buddies in the locker room, as we call it, but it's so difficult to keep the room clean. There have been many times where Easton, the youngest, will have his friend Max over and about fifteen minutes later, they have pulled everything out of all the drawers, out of the closet, and destroyed the room.

Blane and Mason get pretty upset with him, but we let them know that they're accountable for their room.

"If you don't want Easton making the mess," we tell them, "then you guys need to make sure that Easton and his friend pick it up. Don't come running to us."

They have an ownership and responsibility for keeping their room clean even though they didn't make the mess. It's so quick for them to blame everybody else, but ultimately, it's their room, so it's their responsibility. Eventually, they got sick and tired of cleaning up Easton's messes, and so now, they've taken an ownership role of walking in and saying, "Hey, Easton, let's make sure to pick up the room before Max leaves," or they help and now nobody gets in trouble. When I look at my kids with that grand vision of becoming great adults, playing the victim is absolutely one thing that cannot be in the mix. The good news is that when you're responsible for your own actions, you're also accountable for your own success.

Another important trait that's closely tied to personal accountability that I try to diligently instill in my children is being willing to admit you're wrong. If you can do that and openly express that you made a mistake, it's almost physically impossible for the other person to be upset with you. But if you take the opposite approach, if you make excuses or get defensive, it's very easy for the other person to stay mad. I can't think of one circumstance in my life where if I have made a mistake, no matter how big or small, apologized, and let the person know that I messed up, the other person doesn't say, "It's okay. It's not a big deal," and they just let it go. It's amazing how often that happens, and it's a big part of relinquishing the victim mentality. I'm intentional about allowing my kids to see me fail or see me take responsibility so that I can instill the positive trait of accountability in them, and hopefully, they can do the same things when they get older as they grow into adulthood.

IT'S NEVER TOO LATE

I'm led to believe there are fathers out there who are reading this book and thinking, I've made so many mistakes, I don't know where to begin. I haven't been intentional. I haven't done any of these things you're talking about, so how do I start now? I don't know your story and I won't pretend to. I have heard from many fathers who've made some big mistakes like infidelity, drinking and drugging, and some mistakes leading them to divorce or even prison time. I've also heard from plenty of other fathers who simply haven't been engaged or present for their children. We've all made mistakes, myself included, and if you'll allow me to speak into your life for a minute I would appreciate the opportunity. If you're a dad who's saying to himself it's too late, but would like a second chance with his children, let me ask you a question. Who told you that? Seriously, who told you it's too late? I guarantee you it wasn't your children or your wife. It's a lie and one you cannot afford to believe.

I learned the story of a father who fell hard. He was in a prominent position, and alcohol caused him to lose his job and eventually his marriage. He has a daughter he cares about deeply and throughout his entire free fall he never stopped loving her. Their favorite thing to do is go on dates to Waffle House, and they do so regularly. The aspect of his story I love the most is the fact he refused to let the insecurity of his mistakes tarnish the relationship with his daughter. He embraced his second chance, so did his daughter, and your children will too.

The good news is even a small amount of intentionality will have a huge impact, and your family is going to see the most dynamic change because they haven't experienced this version of you in the past or perhaps it's been awhile. If you're a dad who hasn't engaged at this level or hasn't been intentional, this is your chance. It's never too late. You'll be amazed at the response you're going to receive because of just how different your approach is. All it takes are a few small changes because, remember, feelings follow actions—not the other way around. Just starting with a half-hour on the weekend of being intentional and a few minutes here and there during the week of being an active presence in the life of your child will prime the pump to become a better father. It's never too late to start, because kids are resilient. I don't care how old they are, even if they're grown and gone, you still have the opportunity to engage them, and you always have the opportunity to make an impact on them. You're their dad. That position will never be relinquished. Don't let insecurities hold you back from the most important role in your life. Don't yield the battleground to anyone or anything. Reclaim the territory in their lives that's been set aside for you as their father and don't ever let it go again.

"DADFIRMATION"

Can I share one of my pet peeves with you? One thing that frustrates me is when a family member comes to visit, they talk about our house or the fact that we put a pool in our backyard. They talk about our careers and our business success. This lights my fuse because to me, "That doesn't matter. If that's your definition of me being successful, then you've missed the mark." That's not what I want to appreciate about my kids when they're adults. I don't want to walk in and say, "Wow, you financially have hit it out of the park! Way to go, dude!" I want to be able to look at them and say, "Wow, what a great marriage you have, what great faith you have, what a great parent you are. I'm so proud of you for those things, the things that matter, and I don't care if you live in an apartment or if you have a mansion." And, yet, that's the definition of success for many people. Let's face it, fatherhood can be a lonely place at times, and the rewards feel like they are not aligned with what matters most.

In order to provide my children the right affirmation later in life, they need to know what true success looks like along the way. When I set the vision for my children, I'm not setting the vision for what a ten-year-old or an eighteen-year-old looks like. I'm setting a vision for what my kids look like in their twenties, thirties, forties, and beyond. What do I want to see that long-term trajectory look like? What do I need to do today as a father to help get them to that point? As a father you have the power to change a short-term view of fatherhood to a long-range view, looking farther out and saying, "What are the character traits I want my adult children to have? What are the situations in life my kids are going to come up against as adults? Not as children, but as adults, and how can I help prepare them and have those experiences now so that when they get there, they succeed?" Like the Spartan Races have taught me, when I come up against an obstacle, I climb over it or I run through it. I don't turn around and go the other direction. I'm able to push through those hard moments. It's those character traits like grit, loyalty, and determination I want my kids to have when they become great adults.

When you break from the norm in your parenting, you will separate your children from the sea of sameness. I want my kids to be seen as uncommon, which is already occurring. If I can create an uncommon pattern as a child, that will translate to them being uncommon as an adult, and if they're uncommon, it means that when the world comes up against them, or they come up against the world, people will be curious and say, "Hmm, why are Hayden, Blane, Mason, or Easton so different? What makes them act the way that they do?" My goal is that people ask those questions about my children when they're adults because of who they are, not what they do. Having someone come up to me and ask what did you do to raise such a great young man or woman is all the "dadfirmation" I need.

OLD WOODEN TABLE

We don't watch much TV, but when we do we like to watch a show on Netflix called *Blue Bloods*, which stars Tom Selleck and his incredible mustache as the police commissioner of New York City. It's a multigenerational drama that started airing in 2010. Selleck's dad was also the police chief, and his three grown children are all in law enforcement, as well. Every Sunday, they all come back together and sit down at this big table for a family dinner. It's been a lot of fun to watch as the family expands and new faces come to the table as the characters get married or children come along. The family continues to expand and the table gets bigger. It's a very wholesome show that Heather and I enjoy watching together. The show has helped me solidify my long-term vision as a father, where I become the sage at the head of the table, which expands with four amazing adult children and their spouses and children.

While I recognize that the goal of all of them living close by or having dinner every Sunday as a family may not necessarily happen, I've always envisioned that long farm table with my family expanding over time. In fact, that table is a part of my family today where my kids do arts and crafts and their homework and so many other things. My vision is that all the marks and etchings from those years are still there when they come back as adults, and we're all gathered around it. God willing, none have left us. That table is the centerpiece of the vision in my mind for what I want my family dynamics to be later on in life. As I work toward that goal of raising good kids who become great adults, I've got the fixture of that solid oak table in my mind as a symbol of our strength and longevity. I want to be able to sit at the end of it with Heather and just silently look around the table and smile, seeing the fruits of our labor and how all our intentionality paid off. We raised good kids who became great adults. I can simply look at her and them without saying a word and know that all the memory burns, all the time we spent together, prepared them to succeed and to thrive. Maybe it's not an old wooden farm table for you, but what is the symbol you're going to hold close to create the mental picture of your future family state?

CALL TO ACTION

When I first started Daddy Saturday it was simply because I saw the benefit in my own family and children. I started to look outside of my family, realized my calling and discovered the opportunity to disrupt fatherhood and impact the future of our country, and I knew I couldn't do it alone. I needed other core fathers to join me on this journey and together we could create monumental change by eliminating the fatherlessness epidemic. I formed the Daddy Saturday Foundation, a 501(c)(3) non-profit organization, with the goal of impacting 10 million men in the next ten years. People often ask me if I'm overwhelmed by such a large goal and I always answer the same way. I say, "While I have a goal to reach 10 million fathers, I'm not worried about reaching millions. I know if I take care of the father in the mirror and then the individual father in front of me, in the moment God can do more than we could ever ask or imagine!"

If you desire to align yourself with other fathers who share the same beliefs and have a similar velocity in the way they approach fatherhood, then I encourage you to join the countless other fathers in the Daddy Saturday movement. You will be provided with some additional ways to engage with the Daddy Saturday community at the end of the book. Before we get there, I want to challenge you to not only implement the Daddy Saturday principles with your family, but to become an advocate for fatherhood in your community. Become one of the core fathers mentioned above by serving as a Daddy Saturday *Coach* in your community. Let's work together to create inspiring and epic events for fathers and their children to engage in across the globe.

I may not know everything there is to know about fatherhood, but I do know one thing: we as men and as fathers can't sit back and do *nothing*. We cannot fail fatherhood.

Our children's future is too important, and the need for intentional fathers is too urgent.

My call to all fathers is that they create an image of being intentional and engaged with their kids in their minds, whatever that looks like for them, recognizing the fact that it's not going to be easy to get there. It's an uphill battle, but it's a battle worth fighting. I encourage, I implore, I challenge every father out there to start taking the first step toward that goal no matter where you're at in the process. I'm here to help you, as is the rest of the Daddy Saturday community. Life's a journey, and there are going to be twists and turns, and ups and downs, and peaks and valleys. Even with everything I've shared with you I still have days where I don't feel like being intentional or I fail miserably as a father. Those days may never show up on my dad résumé and they most likely won't show up on yours, yet it's how you rebound from those days that truly makes the measure of a father. Recognize that there will be fears and insecurities that never fully dissipate from your psyche, but as an intentional father you've got what it takes to drown them out with your vision and values.

We may be in a sour state of fatherhood, but I'm not willing to go down without a fight, and I know as fathers we can create a paradigm shift so powerful through the Daddy Saturday movement it changes the trajectory of our society for decades to come. Who's with me? I can't promise this will be easy, but I can assure you it will be worth it. The time is now and this is your defining moment as a father. The ripples in the pond will go way beyond your family. The butterfly effect will take hold and our children will affect so many other people and become productive members of society because of our investment in them as intentional fathers. Join the Daddy Saturday movement and help me craft the story of how a father can change the world...

One Daddy Saturday at a time.

ABOUT THE AUTHOR

JUSTIN BATT aims to disrupt fatherhood with *intentionality*, by creating intentional fathers who raise good kids who become great adults. He founded Daddy Saturday in his own backyard with his four children, and it's grown into a national movement engaging fathers across multiple channels, including YouTube, social media, the *Daddy Saturday* book, an Alexa skill, a podcast, merchandise, live events, and a 501(c)(3) foundation, through which Justin plans to impact 10 million fathers in the next 10 years.

In addition, Justin is a highly sought after healthcare consultant and a successful serial entrepreneur, as well as a TEDx and international public speaker, a multi-published author, and a regular guest on multiple podcasts. When not at work, Justin can be found helping his wife, Heather, run her bridal enterprise, and spending time with his four children and the family's Bernedoodle, Weekend.

Me and my ACE

Join the **Daddy Saturday** Movement by
giving to the **Daddy Saturday** Foundation,
a 501(c)(3) non-profit organization.

Help us end the fatherlessness epidemic
by reaching our goal of impacting 10
million fathers in the next 10 years.

Give Now at: **DaddySaturdayFoundation.com**

Visit **DaddySaturday.com** for information
on how to become a Daddy Saturday
Coach in your local community.

Visit **DaddySaturday.com/bonus**
for exclusive access to all of the free
resources mentioned in the book!